Christian Heroes: Then & Now

# William Carey

## Obliged to Go

CHRISTIAN HEROES: THEN & NOW

# WILLIAM CAREY

## Obliged to Go

JANET & GEOFF BENGE

YWAM Publishing is the publishing ministry of Youth With A Mission (YWAM), an international missionary organization of Christians from many denominations dedicated to presenting Jesus Christ to this generation. To this end, YWAM has focused its efforts in three main areas: (1) training and equipping believers for their part in fulfilling the Great Commission (Matthew 28:19), (2) personal evangelism, and (3) mercy ministry (medical and relief work).

For a free catalog of books and materials, call (425) 771-1153 or (800) 922-2143. Visit us online at www.ywampublishing.com.

**William Carey: Obliged to Go**


Published by YWAM Publishing
a ministry of Youth With A Mission
P.O. Box 55787, Seattle, WA 98155-0787



ISBN 978-1-57658-147-6 (paperback)
ISBN 978-1-57658-569-6 (e-book)

Thirteenth printing 2024

Printed in the United States of America

# Christian Heroes: Then & Now

Adoniram Judson
Albert Schweitzer
Amy Carmichael
Betty Greene
Brother Andrew
Cameron Townsend
Charles Mulli
Clarence Jones
Corrie ten Boom
Count Zinzendorf
C. S. Lewis
C. T. Studd
David Bussau
David Livingstone
Dietrich Bonhoeffer
D. L. Moody
Elisabeth Elliot
Eric Liddell
Florence Young
Francis Asbury
George Müller
Gladys Aylward
Helen Roseveare
Hudson Taylor
Ida Scudder
Isobel Kuhn
Jacob DeShazer
Jim Elliot
John Flynn
John Newton
John Wesley
John Williams
Jonathan Goforth
Klaus-Dieter John
Lillian Trasher
Loren Cunningham
Lottie Moon
Mary Slessor
Mildred Cable
Nate Saint
Norman Grubb
Paul Brand
Rachel Saint
Richard Wurmbrand
Rowland Bingham
Samuel Zwemer
Sundar Singh
Wilfred Grenfell
William Booth
William Carey

This book is dedicated to
John and Shirley Baker,
true pioneers in their own right.

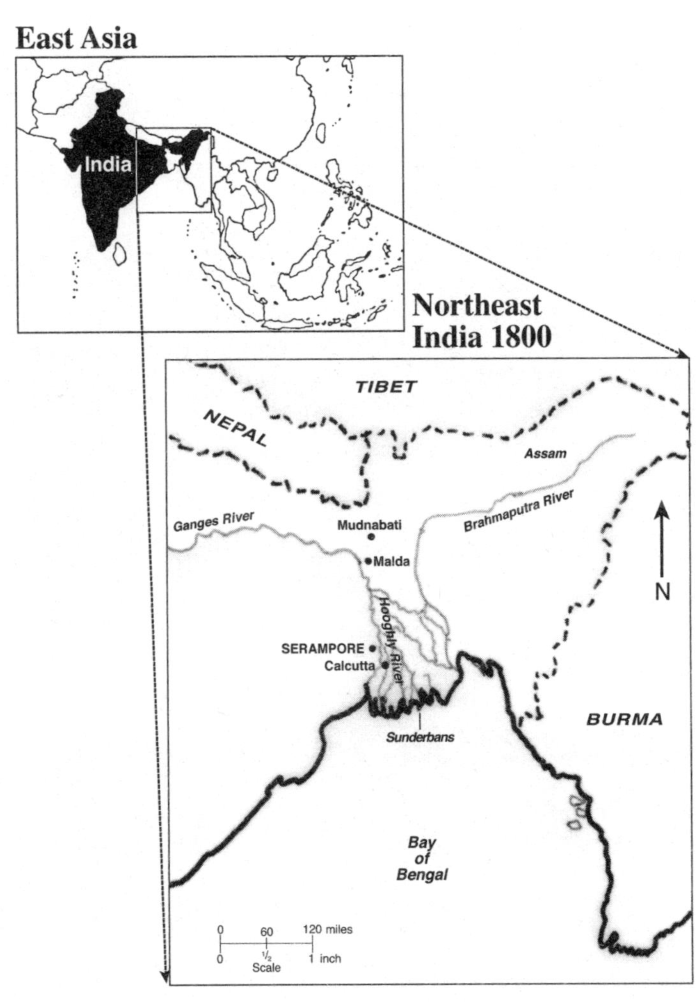
East Asia
India
Northeast
India 1800
TIBET
NEPAL
Assam
Brahmaputra River
Ganges River
Mudnabati
Malda
Hooghly River
SERAMPORE
Calcutta
Sunderbans
BURMA
N
Bay
of
Bengal
0
60
120 miles
0
1/2
1 inch
Scale

## Contents

Chapter 1

# Sailing Away Without Him

William Carey stared at the pile of wooden crates and leather trunks that had been dumped onto the Portsmouth dock beside the *Earl of Oxford.* He recalled the excitement he had felt as his belongings were loaded onto the ship in London a month earlier. An adventure had laid ahead for him and his oldest son, Felix. Now the dream was shattered. The two of them stood side by side on the dock, watching the ship being made ready to sail, only this time it was going to sail without them.

As sailors scurried up and down the rigging, William begged Captain White to reconsider. The captain would not. It simply wasn't worth his career to take unlicensed passengers to India.

An hour later, the *Earl of Oxford* cast off and drifted away from the dock. As she did so, the crew hoisted her sails into position. William squeezed Felix tightly beside him, knowing that his son wouldn't understand what was happening. How could he? William could hardly make sense of it himself. The *Earl of Oxford* had set sail for India without them.

William watched as the vessel joined the other six ships that would form the convoy. Despite his disappointment, William was captivated by the magnificent sight of white sails flapping in the afternoon's soft, spring sunlight. The ships headed down Portsmouth Harbor toward the English Channel. A tear slid down his cheek as William watched them go.

A thousand questions and doubts flooded William's mind as the ships sailed toward the horizon. Had the British and French not been at war, William and his son wouldn't have had to stop in Portsmouth in the first place. Instead, they would be halfway to India by now. Or if they had sailed a day earlier from London, they would have been able to sail with the earlier convoy and not wait for a month while a new one was assembled. And what was going to happen now? William had been commissioned and sent out as a missionary to India, but instead he was stuck in Portsmouth. What would he tell the missionary society now? Would he ever get to India?

As the ships slid over the horizon, William turned his back on the sea. He hired a small cart to take their belongings to the boardinghouse where he and Felix were staying. As he walked alongside the cart, he thought about how far he'd come from the small boy growing up in Paulerspury. But he still had a long way to go. He had to get to India, and he had to get there soon. He knew there was much work for him to do in that far-off place.

Chapter 2

# The Flitting

"William. William. It's time for the flitting," a woman's voice called across the open field.

"Coming, Mother," called back six-year-old William Carey as he swung himself down from the oak tree he had been climbing, being very careful not to rip his pants like he had done the week before. Once safely on the ground, William ran eagerly across the field in the direction of the gray stone cottage, where he'd lived all his young life. Before entering the cottage, he brushed some twigs from his shoulder-length brown hair and straightened his collar. Even during a flitting, his mother expected him to look tidy. When he was satisfied that he would pass inspection, he stepped excitedly inside. He'd dreamed of this moment for weeks, and now it was finally about to happen.

Paulerspury, in the heart of the midlands of England, was not a particularly exciting place for a six-year-old boy, or anyone else for that matter, in 1767. About eight hundred people lived in the town. They were mostly humble folk, like William's parents, Edmund and Elizabeth Carey, who ran a small business in their tiny cottage from which they barely made enough money to feed their growing family. William's parents were both weavers and spent their days, and a good part of their nights, weaving a woolen cloth called "tammy," which was then sold to middlemen who traded it in London. At least, that's how things had been up until today. But today, things were going to change. Today was the day of the flitting. Everything in William's life was about to change, and William knew it.

Flitting was the eighteenth-century name for moving house, and as he stepped inside the cottage, William found his father and the church rector carrying the family's sturdy table and chairs outside into the bright summer sun. As they did so, William thought about all the changes his father's being appointed the clerk of the Church of St. James the Great would bring. (The Church of St. James the Great was part of the Church of England, the only religion officially recognized by King George III.)

William was most excited about the opportunity he would have to go to school. Up until this point, it had been out of the question for him to think of attending a private school. There wasn't enough money in the house to buy new shoes for everyone, let alone to pay for schooling. In England at that time, there were few free schools. As a result, most villagers did not know how to read or write, and most of them had little need to anyway. Thankfully, though, the town of Paulerspury was different from most towns. Two very rich men who had grown up there and then moved away to make their fortunes in London had sent back enough money for the church to set up a free school in the village for twelve children. Since Edmund Carey was to be the new church clerk, William was given one of the places in the school. Of course, while attending school, he would be seeing a lot of his father, since one of the clerk's duties was to be the schoolmaster.

William's father's new job also meant a change in housing, hence the flitting. Up until then, William, his four-year-old sister Ann, and his parents had all been squeezed into the two tiny rooms that made up their weaver's cottage. The loom had filled nearly all of the downstairs room. From a young age, William and Ann had learned how to play around the loom while avoiding their parents' elbows and knees as they operated the weaving monstrosity. But now they would be moving out of the small, damp cottage at Pury End on the western end of the mile-long village to Church End, across the bubbling stream that divided the town in half. There they would move into the house that came with their father's new job.

This house was a two-story thatched cottage with two fireplaces and four lattice windows in the front. Compared to what they had been living in, it was a palace. The move came just in time, too, because William's mother was expecting another baby any day. While there was no room for another child, not even a tiny baby, in their weaver's cottage, the new house was much bigger, so much so that William was going to have his own bedroom. He would be one of the few children in town who had a room all to himself.

Of course, William knew exactly how he was going to fill it. Even at six, he had collected more things than most adults do in a lifetime. Not things that cost money, but natural things from all around him. He would go on long walks in the Royal Whittlebury Forest that grew to the edge of the village. He loved to wander under the enormous oak trees looking for crickets, worms, bird's eggs, and butterflies, which he could add to his collection. If he saw an unfamiliar insect, he would dive into the hawthorn undergrowth to capture it. Some of the things he found were dead, and some were alive. He brought them all back home and kept them in little wooden boxes and cages his father had made for him. As he carried the washboard and a leather bucket along the road to his new house, William planned out how he would arrange all his treasures in the new bedroom.

Before night fell, everything had been moved, including many of William's favorite plants that he had dug up from the old house and replanted under his bedroom window. When he went to bed that first night in his new bedroom, the scent of his favorite rosebush was just outside his window to keep him company.

William quickly grew used to his new life, though there was one thing he didn't like about it. During Sunday services at the Church of St. James the Great, William had to sit with his family in a special gallery behind the pulpit from which the Reverend Jones preached his long sermons. True, it was fun to be higher than everyone else, and William could see over everyone's head, all the way to the bell ringers who stood at the back of the church. But although he could see all that was going on, at the same time, he felt he was on display. His mother constantly reminded him to mind his manners because everyone was watching. During services, many of his school friends would make faces at him from the pews. William had to try his hardest to ignore them. He knew he'd be punished if he dared return their looks. Unless he had to stay home and watch over his new baby sister, Polly (her real name was Mary, but no one ever called her that), William was in church every Sunday.

William's father had several special duties to perform during Sunday services. He led the congregation in prayers and chants and announced the sermon. He was also responsible for making sure that the church was kept clean and that dogs did not run through it. As well, he entered births and deaths in the church register. While the church itself did not pay him much, he was allowed to keep the fee he charged for making entries in the register.

While the family still did not have much money to spare, there was one thing about his father's new job that excited William—the books. There were few books printed in England in the 1760s. Producing a single book during this period was time-consuming and expensive. As a result, most books were owned by rich people and clergymen. But now that his father was both schoolmaster and the church clerk, William got to know many people who loaned him books. He was a quick learner, and it was not long before he was engrossed in the adventure stories of the day, such as *Robinson Crusoe* and *Gulliver's Travels.* And not just adventure stories. William read everything he could get his hands on, especially books about foreign lands. Such books fired his imagination. Often when he was alone, he would pretend to be Sir Francis Drake passing through the Straits of Magellan in the *Golden Hind,* or Christopher Columbus sailing off to discover new worlds in the name of Ferdinand and Isabella, the king and queen of Spain. In fact, some friends found William acting out Columbus discovering America one day and nicknamed him "Columbus," a nickname that stuck with him into adulthood.

William's love of foreign lands was also fueled when his long-lost Uncle Peter returned from Canada, where he had fought against the French, helping to capture the province of Quebec for the British Empire. No one had ever thought that Uncle

Peter would come home again, but one fall day, he just showed up in Paulerspury with amazing tales to tell of where he had been and the things he'd seen. He had fought alongside General James Wolfe and traded with Algonquin Indians.

The now eight-year-old William was fascinated by his Uncle Peter and asked him to tell and retell his many stories. He especially liked to hear about the sea voyage across the Atlantic Ocean. Even though he had pretended to be Sir Francis Drake and Christopher Columbus, William had always had difficulty trying to imagine what the ocean really looked like. Uncle Peter told him to think of it as a million streams all running side by side and stretching as far as the eye could see. William tried to imagine, just like he tried to imagine a city as huge as London with six hundred thousand people living in it. But try as he may, it was not easy to imagine for a young boy who'd never been more than ten miles away from the country village where he had been born.

William spent many hours with Uncle Peter, who had no family of his own. Besides being a wonderful source of information about the world, Uncle Peter knew a lot about plants. In fact, soon after his return to Paulerspury, he was hired by the village squire to be a gardener. From then on, whenever William and his uncle got together, they would discuss their gardens and often swapped plant cuttings, bulbs, and gardening hints.

Life seemed to go well for William, who loved school, though his father was tougher on him than the other students. William also loved being outside in his garden, which soon became one of the best in the village. His little sister Polly followed him nearly everywhere he went, so William made her his "research assistant" and let her carry the bag that he filled with plant and animal specimens when they went walking together. Sometimes on these walks, William would carry along his new baby brother, Tom, but not for too long. Tom grew quickly and was soon too heavy to carry.

William was interested in all sorts of things, and although he lived in a tiny village ten miles south of Northampton, the newspaper gave him a glimpse of the world beyond Paulerspury. The *Northampton Mercury* was published every Monday, and three copies of the paper were delivered to Paulerspury by a postboy on horseback. One copy of the newspaper went to the church rector, one to the squire, and the third to the schoolmaster. William could hardly wait for the paper to arrive each week. There were so many amazing things happening in the world to read about. In 1764, James Hargreave invented a machine for spinning eight strands of thread at a time. He named the machine after his daughter, calling it the spinning jenny. Then in 1769, Richard Arkwright improved on this invention and developed a spinning machine that would make stronger yarn than the spinning jenny. Arkwright then built large mills to house his spinning machines and used steam engines, invented in 1765 by James Watt, to power the pumps to supply the water to turn the waterwheel that ran the spinning machines. In 1769, a Frenchman, Nicolas Cugnot, used Watt's steam engine to power a motorized carriage. William read about all these things in the newspaper.

In 1771, the *Northampton Mercury* celebrated the return to England of Captain James Cook and the crew of the *Endeavor*. Cook had sailed to Tahiti to observe the transit of Venus and explore the west coast of Australia, as well as to map the coast of New Zealand. William carefully saved the pages from the newspaper that contained excerpts from Cook's diaries. He would read and reread the accounts of the various natives Cook had met along the way.

One day, when William had read all the other books in the house, he began looking through some books Uncle Peter had left there. One of the books was a huge volume that contained many sketches of plants. There was just one problem: Eleven-year-old William couldn't read any of the words in the book. He realized they must be in a foreign language, though he had no idea what language. Uncle Peter had uttered a few words in French that he'd remembered from his time in Canada, but apart from that, William had no idea what any language other than English sounded like or what it might look like written down.

William thought his father might know more about the language. Sure enough, Edmund Carey knew it was Latin, the same Latin that was engraved on some of the oldest gravestones and tombs around the Church of St. James the Great. Mr. Carey didn't know how to read Latin himself, but he had noticed an old copy of a Latin grammar book tucked up on a shelf in the schoolhouse. He dusted the book off and gave it to William.

Within a couple of months, William had memorized the entire book and spoke enough Latin to hold a conversation, though he had to talk to himself! Best of all, though, he could now read for himself the text that went along with the pictures of plants in Uncle Peter's book.

The village school taught boys only up to the age of twelve. After twelve, the boys either had to go to the city to enroll in a more advanced school or had to hire a private tutor. Unfortunately, the Careys did not have the money to do either. So, like the other boys in the village, at twelve years of age, William had to find a job and help support the family.

Seventeen seventy-two, the year William finished school, was also the year that tensions between the American colonies and the British began to grow. Some people wondered how the colonists thought they could possibly win their independence without a king to lead them into battle. Others fretted that the French might get involved and help the colonists, to get even with the English for taking Quebec from them. All this made for some lively debates in the schoolroom, but William was no longer there to take part in them. Instead, he was working as a farm laborer.

Although William had enough education to get an indoor job, he loved to be outdoors so much that he had begged his father to find him a job outside. William went to work on a farm. Although he had a slight build and was small for his age, he proved to be a hard worker. He ploughed the fields in preparation for planting the crops, and he tended the Leicester sheep, which spent their days on the rolling green hills of the countryside.

Although William loved being out in the sun, the sun did not love him. He developed an allergy to it that the village herb doctor was unable to cure. Whenever it was sunny, William got a painful rash on his face and hands. But because he longed so much to work outside with animals and plants, he put up with the pain of the rash for two years. In the end, though, he had to admit to himself that it was too difficult to go on. William would have to find another job.

Although William didn't know it at the time, the rash on his face would change the course of his life. Had it not been for the rash, William may well have lived his whole life and died in Paulerspury. The search for a new job, however, took him ten miles away from his home—the first ten miles on a journey that would rival any of the adventures he'd read about in *Gulliver's Travels* or *Robinson Crusoe.*

## Chapter 3

# The Apprentice

William's father had to make a decision. What job should he find for his oldest son? Most people assumed that Edmund Carey would apprentice his son to a weaver, just as he had been apprenticed as a young man. But Mr. Carey was not so sure. There had been a lot of news in the *Northampton Mercury* over the past year about how the new spinning machines and steam-driven weaving looms were about to change the way fabric was made. Many people in Paulerspury argued that fabric had been made by hand in small cottages for generations and that was the way it would always be made. William's father wasn't so sure, though. He thought that steam-powered factories would soon be able to spin yarn and weave fabric a hundred times faster than a single weaver at his loom. And then where would weavers be? It might not be such a wise idea, he decided, to apprentice William to a weaver.

So if William could no longer work outside and wasn't going to be a weaver, what should he do? The question hung in the air for several days, until Edmund Carey heard that a cordwainer named Clarke Nichols was looking for an apprentice. A cordwainer was a person who made shoes from scratch. The job included making shoe "forms" out of wooden blocks, cutting the leather to shape, and stitching it together. This all took a lot of skill, much more skill than it took to be a cobbler, a person who mended shoes for a living.

Clarke Nichols lived in Piddington, a town eight miles northeast of Paulerspury. Edmund Carey made the trek there to visit Mr. Nichols. The two men talked for a while and then shook hands. Mr. Carey walked home quickly to tell his son the good news: William was now an apprentice cordwainer.

Being an apprentice was a serious matter in 1774. A young man would sign a contract to learn a trade from a master tradesman. He would then be the master tradesman's apprentice for seven years until he himself became a tradesman. In the seven years it took to learn a trade, an apprentice did not get paid. However, along with teaching the trade to his apprentice, the tradesman fed his apprentice, clothed him, and gave him a place to live. Once signed, the apprenticeship agreement was binding, meaning the apprentice had to obey his master and could not leave until the seven years were up.

For the first time in his life, fourteen-year-old William Carey had to move away from home to work. In a kerchief, his mother packed him a spare shirt, a pair of knitted socks, and a tin plate and cup. The family walked with him out to Whattle Road, which would take him to Piddington. Twelve-year-old Ann and seven-year-old Tom were sad to see him leave, but nine-year-old Polly was heartbroken. She hugged William and promised to look after every item in his specimen collection.

It took William four hours to walk to Piddington. He could have done it faster, but he paused for almost half an hour to watch a barge being pulled down the newly dug canal just outside of Paulerspury. Canals were being dug all over the countryside, and William thought a barge looked like a whole lot more comfortable way to travel. As he walked along, horses galloped by, and a large carriage pulled by four horses also rattled past, but most people on Whattle Road were walking, just as he was. And as people walked past him, William thought how sensible it was to become a cordwainer. People would always be wearing out their shoes on rough roads like the one he was walking on.

It was midafternoon when William finally got to Mr. Nichols's workshop, which was also his cottage. He was met at the door by a tall, dark-haired boy, whom William decided was about three years older than he.

"John Warr is the name," said the boy, introducing himself. "You must be the new apprentice."

William nodded shyly.

"Well, it's about time you showed up. I'm tired of doing all the deliveries myself," said John with a grin.

William smiled. "Anytime you want to send me out for a walk is fine with me," he replied wryly.

William stepped inside the cottage, thinking how much he liked John already. As he had guessed, John Warr was already three years into his apprenticeship. He showed William up the stairs at the back of the workshop and into the attic, where the two of them were to share a room. William looked around at his new bedroom, thinking of where he might ask to put up shelves. He was sure that while making his delivery rounds he'd come up with a whole new collection of specimens to study.

The two boys made their way back downstairs just as Mr. Nichols bustled in the door carrying several newly tanned hides. He spotted William immediately. "Glad you're here, lad," he said. "Your father tells me you're a quick one. We'll soon see if that's true. You can start by picking up the leather scraps and putting them in that bag over there." He pointed to a cloth bag hanging from the back of a chair.

It did not take William long to settle into the routine of work. There was plenty to keep him busy. Being the newest apprentice, he got to do all the worst jobs, like beating the leather to make it more pliable, hammering in rivets, and delivering the finished pairs of shoes. It was on one of these delivery rounds that William made a foolish mistake he would remember for the rest of his life.

It happened around Christmastime. Since an apprentice did not earn money, at Christmas he was often allowed to collect a few pennies in donations from some of the other tradesmen his master bought supplies from. These donations were called a "Christmas Box." One of William's deliveries was a pair of boots to the local blacksmith, who paid William the shilling he owed Mr. Nichols for the boots. Then he asked, "And what would you like for your Christmas Box, lad? Will it be a sixpence or a shilling?"

William could hardly believe his luck! A shilling was a lot of money, enough to buy the new quill pen he'd had his eye on for weeks.

"The shilling, thank you, sir," he replied quickly, before the blacksmith had a chance to change his mind.

The blacksmith chuckled to himself as he handed over the coin, and soon William was out in the snow heading for the store to buy the quill pen.

Inside the store, William pulled from his pocket the shilling he'd been given and handed it to the storekeeper. The storekeeper frowned as he turned it over in his hand. "This here is not a silver shilling, lad," he said sternly. "It's made of brass if ever a coin was. You weren't trying to get the better of me, were you?" The storekeeper peered down at William.

William could feel his face going red. The blacksmith had played a trick on him and given him a counterfeit coin. No wonder he had been chuckling to himself as he handed it over!

The wonderful quill pen sat so temptingly on the shelf, and William had set his heart on using it that evening. In an instant, he knew just what to do. The blacksmith had given him two shillings, one to pay for the boots and one for himself. So why not swap the two coins? Who would know? Quickly, William took back the brass coin and reached into Mr. Nichols's pouch to find the silver shilling.

Within a minute it was done. The brass shilling was back in the pouch, and William was holding the quill pen he'd wanted so badly. All the way back to the workshop, William went over his act. He would look Mr. Nichols right in the eye and smile as he gave him the money pouch. If Mr. Nichols noticed the brass shilling straightaway, William would run over to him and stare at it in wide-eyed amazement. Then he would begin stammering an apology for not noticing the counterfeit coin sooner and promise to look more carefully at every coin given to him in the future.

By the time William stepped through the door, he was sure everything would go just fine. Mr. Nichols was standing at his workbench with hammer in hand, tacking the leather sole onto a boot. He put the hammer down as William came through the door, letting in a blast of cold air behind him.

"The blacksmith and the rector both paid in full," said William matter-of-factly as he handed the money pouch to his employer. He could feel his heart thumping hard, but he knew how to look calm on the outside. William turned to get the broom, as the floor was in need of sweeping.

Mr. Nichols reached into the pouch and pulled out the brass coin. "What's this?" he asked gruffly. "Who gave you this shilling?"

"The blacksmith," replied William looking up innocently. "Is there a problem with it?"

"A problem! Yes, there is a problem. The coin is a counterfeit," Mr. Nichols said. Then he yelled, "John! John, come here. I have a job for you."

John came hurrying in from out back where he had been unloading a bail of newly tanned hides.

"The blacksmith has given William a brass shilling. He probably thought the lad was too stupid to notice. It seems he was," said Mr. Nichols to John while staring straight at William. "Take the coin back and demand a good one in its place." He tossed the coin to John.

John pulled his coat tight around him and walked out into the cold. A chilling wind whipped in the door, but it was not as cold as the chill that wrapped itself around William's heart.

William went back to sweeping the floor, but he could hardly concentrate on the simple task. Why hadn't he thought that Mr. Nichols might go back to the blacksmith? What would happen if the truth came out? He hated to think about the answer. There was no doubt that stealing a shilling was a serious offense—very serious, in fact. The punishment for stealing a shilling or less was either imprisonment, a public whipping, or being shipped off to one of the king's plantations in America or the West Indies to work for seven years. The only thing William could comfort himself with was the fact that it was only a shilling he had stolen. The punishment for stealing more than a shilling was death by public hanging, after which the thief's corpse would often be left at the side of a well-traveled road as a warning to others not to steal. William had occasionally passed such corpses while making his deliveries. The message not to steal, however, hadn't seemed to sink in.

William began to pray. "Oh, God, if You get me out of this, I will never lie again. I'll go to church three times every Sunday, and I will never steal another thing. Just get me out of this. I don't want to go to the West Indies."

When the blacksmith himself came back with John a half hour later, it seemed to William Carey that God was not going to answer his desperate prayer. The whole story came tumbling out. The blacksmith explained to Mr. Nichols that he had given William the brass coin for his Christmas Box as a joke and he was surprised when William had not noticed right away that it was fake. William apologized and begged Mr. Nichols to forgive him. He promised to repay the shilling with the rest of his Christmas Box money. Finally, Mr. Nichols had compassion for him and agreed not to take him to the magistrate. It was a quiet Christmas for William, who was very grateful not to be on his way to the West Indies as a criminal!

As he worked, William was never without a book of some sort close by. As he tapped tacks into the sole of a shoe, he would glance up every few strokes of the hammer and read a line or two from the book he had propped open on his workbench. Mr. Nichols didn't seem to mind his doing this, since William still managed to finish all his work.

Mr. Nichols liked books himself and had several in his home. One afternoon, William picked up one of Mr. Nichols's books to read. As he opened it, he saw that it was filled with row upon row of beautiful squiggles and curly figures. This strange text fascinated him. He could not read a word of it and wasn't even sure what language it was.

William was curious about the book and decided to investigate. He knew just the person to ask. It was rumored that Thomas Jones, an old weaver in the village of Paulerspury, had been to university—a rare thing in those days. William felt sure that Thomas Jones would know something about what language it was. On one of his few days off, William hurried back to his hometown to visit Mr. Jones. He was well rewarded. Mr. Jones took one look at the book and chuckled to himself. He explained to William that the book was written in Greek, and he began translating some of the words. William was fascinated by the language and asked so many questions that, in the end, Mr. Jones offered to teach him the language.

Mr. Jones later told William that he had expected him to give up after a lesson or two. After all, why would an apprentice cordwainer want to know Greek? But Mr. Jones didn't know William! For two years, William studied Greek every spare moment he had, and by the end of that time, he could read and write the language well. By the time he was sixteen years old, William was one of the better educated men in the district. He had no idea that one day he would use this knowledge to help people half a world away.

Since William had not been shipped off to the West Indies for swapping the brass shilling, he kept his promise and began attending church three times each Sunday. He often talked about church with John Warr. Both men loved to argue about religion. William's father was an Anglican church clerk, and John's father was a leader in a nonconformist church. (Nonconformists were also called "dissenters" and belonged to Baptist, Congregational, Presbyterian, and Quaker denominations.) Most of the discussions between William and John centered around the different ways their fathers' churches worshiped. The two friends had extensive disagreements over everything from infant baptism to who should qualify as a minister. Often the discussions would turn into heated arguments.

William was very good at arguing and "won" nearly every religious argument he had with John. Sometimes he had the uncomfortable feeling that even when he had won an argument, he'd lost something a lot more important, but he could never admit that to John.

Secretly, William admired John for being a nonconformist. A person had to be willing to make sacrifices to be one. For example, the Test and Corporation Acts barred dissenters from being paid officers of the state and from holding rank in the army or navy. William was also aware that the children of dissenters were banned from going to the school in Paulerspury. To be a dissenter was definitely to be outside the mainstream of eighteenth-century English life.

Still, William would not let John get the better of him in an argument. In one argument, John maintained that the Church of England was not free to do as God wanted, since its main job was to serve and please the king, who was automatically the head of the church. In John's opinion, this made the state church nothing more than a pawn. Little did either of them know that an event was unfolding across the Atlantic Ocean that would force William to come to the same conclusion.

The event was the American Revolution. William had followed events in America closely ever since his Uncle Peter had come back from fighting in Canada. Actually, it was the British winning the war against the French in Quebec that had helped bring on the American Revolution. Once Canada was firmly under British control, the American colonists were no longer afraid that France would invade them from the north. Without this threat of invasion, many of the English troops stationed in America were sent home. The colonists had been willing to pay high taxes to the king for protection against the French, but now that the soldiers were gone, the colonists began to ask each other why they still had to pay the same high taxes. What was the king doing for them that they could not do for themselves? Thus, in 1775, the colonists had rebelled at the Battle of Lexington and signed a declaration of independence from Britain the following year. Spain and France had declared that they would fight for America's freedom, and so the American Revolution had raged on.

George Washington, whose grandparents were from Northhamptonshire, and the "rebel" colonists became the champions of a lot of people in Piddington and Paulerspury. Many people in the area said that King George III was mad and unable to make wise decisions and that they should all be praying for a new king rather than for the failure of George Washington and the rebels in America. William was also beginning to think this way. As he had read about the situation, he'd come to the conclusion that the cause of the American colonists was right and just.

For many months, John Warr had been inviting William to go with him to the meetinghouse at Shackleton, but William had always refused, that is, until King George III declared Wednesday, February 10, 1779, to be a national day of prayer and fasting. Things were going badly for Britain in many other parts of the world besides the American colonies. France and Spain had declared war on

England, and their warships were in the English channel, waiting for the right moment to strike. In India, British troops were being attacked by well-organized bands of locals, and in the West Indies, France was fighting a sea battle with the English navy.

William wanted to take part in the day of prayer for his country—every Englishman did—but he could not bring himself to pray for the downfall of the revolutionary troops in America. Instead, he hoped they won! Feeling this way meant that he couldn't go to the Anglican prayer service, where the king had ordered all worshipers to pray for the defeat of the American rebels. The dissenters, on the other hand, were praying for the revolutionaries to win. William thus made up his mind to accept John Warr's invitation to the nonconformist prayer service.

William Carey had no idea what a different world he was about to enter. Nor could he have known the effect he would have on that world in years to come!

Chapter 4

# Among the Dissenters

William didn't quite know what to expect as he stepped through the low door of the meeting hall. He had heard that the dissenters had strange habits, and he promised himself he would keep his guard up. But as the meeting progressed, he felt strangely at home. Several men gave short messages, and others stood to read verses from the Bible. William had never been in a group of people who seemed to believe what they read with such certainty. One of the men in the group, Mr. Chater of Hackleton, read some verses from Hebrews chapter 13: "Let us go forth therefore unto him without the camp, bearing his reproach."

William felt that the words spoke directly to him. He had spent his whole life going to the right church, saying the right things, being in the "fashionable" camp. Despite all this, he had not felt any power to change who he was. Now he began to think that maybe he belonged outside the camp—outside the state religion and among the dissenters. It was a startling thought to William, but he knew it was right. When the prayer meeting was over, he talked to John Warr about the decision he'd made. He wanted to become a dissenter!

John was excited and enthusiastic. Now he and William had even longer discussions as they cut soles and sewed seams. They took turns reading chapters of the Bible aloud while the other one hammered and sewed shoes.

For the next six months, things went along quite smoothly for William, until September 1779. That month, William's master, Clarke Nichols, died suddenly, leaving both William and John without a job. By then, John had finished his apprenticeship and was able to find work quickly, but William still had two years to go on his apprenticeship. After several weeks of searching, Thomas Old of Hackleton agreed to take William in to finish his apprenticeship.

William moved two miles away to Hackleton, where he began attending a dissenter church headed by a Mr. Plackett, who had three daughters. The middle daughter was called Dolly, though her real name was Dorothy. She and William were often together at the dissenter services. Dolly also visited the Old home often because her elder sister was married to Thomas Old, William's new boss.

While Dolly was six years older than William, she was quiet and shy. William, on the other hand, had an opinion on everything. Soon the two of them were "walking out together," as dating was then called; and in June 1781, less than two years after William had moved to Hackelton, they were married. William was nineteen years old and could barely afford a wife, since he was still an apprentice.

The wedding was small. Dolly's younger sister, Kitty, was the bridesmaid, and when it came time to sign the marriage register, both Dolly and Kitty signed with an *X*. Neither of them had been to school and so had never been taught to write. This was not unusual for women during this period. William promised to teach Dolly to read and write after they were married.

At first, the marriage went well. The couple lived in a tiny cottage, and William put all his spare time into creating two gardens: one to grow vegetables and the other to grow the flowers he loved so much. Within a year, their first child, a daughter, was born. William named her Ann, after his grandmother who had died when he was very young. Now William had not only a wife but also a child to support on the small wage he earned from his shoemaking.

During his second year in Hackleton, William had become a part-time preacher for the dissenters and spoke every two weeks at the village of Earls Barton, eight miles away. Of course, he had to walk there and back. The people in the church were poor mat makers and couldn't even afford to pay him enough to buy the leather to make a new pair of shoes to replace the ones he wore out with all the walking.

William also preached once a month at Paulerspury, where he would stop at his parents' house for lunch after the service. William's mother was very proud when the neighbors told her what a wonderful preacher her son was. None of the family members dared go and hear him themselves, however. It would not be right for a clerk of the Church of England or anyone living in his house to be seen at a dissenter service. It would cost William's father his job if he attended such a meeting.

William's parents had not made the ten-mile walk to see William at his new home in Hackleton, so they had no idea how little money he and Dolly really had. William's family often ate oatmeal and water for days at a time. When their daughter, Ann, was eighteen months old and just starting to talk, she became very ill. William and Dolly did their best to help her, but she soon died. William also became very sick with the same illness and was not able to attend Ann's funeral. A message was sent to his mother, who came to help the sad household.

When Elizabeth Carey arrived at her son's house, she was appalled to see the conditions he and Dolly were living in. It was no wonder the baby had died and William was deathly ill. The cottage was so damp that the pages of William's books were all limp. There was no food in the larder and not enough warm bed coverings to keep a person from freezing on a snowy night.

Mrs. Carey set right to work scrubbing down the moldy walls and boiling a huge pot of soup. As she worked, Dolly sat limply in the corner beside William's bed, unable to believe what was happening. Was she to lose her baby daughter and her husband all in the same week?

With his mother's special care, William slowly began to recover, but not completely. For the rest of his life, he caught coughs and colds easily, and often he had a sore chest, especially when the weather was cold and damp. There was one other side effect of his illness. When William got up from his sickbed, the top of his head was completely bald. All that was left were little tufts of hair around his ears. He kept waiting for the rest of his hair to grow back, but in the end, he gave up hope and ordered a cheap wig from Mr. Wilson, a wigmaker and fellow dissenter in Olney. William was only twenty-three at the time and was very embarrassed about being bald, especially when he was invited to preach somewhere new.

Although William was bald and had a delicate chest as a result of his sickness, something much worse had happened to Dolly, who had gone into shock with baby Ann's death. Although she eventually went back to cleaning and cooking, something inside her had died. She'd lost the sparkle in her eyes.

It took many weeks before William was well enough to go back to working full time, and without his working, the family had no money to buy food. William's younger brother, Tom, had generously sent over the money he'd been saving from his own small income. The money kept William and Dolly from starving. When Mrs. Carey returned to Paulerspury and explained the situation to her friends and neighbors, many of them gave money until there was enough for William and Dolly to buy a tiny cottage in Piddington. The cottage was located on higher ground than their previous cottage and was not so damp. Dolly was glad to move. Everything in the old cottage reminded her of the daughter she had just buried. William hoped that the new house would mean a fresh start for them both. But even after the move, Dolly still couldn't get the thought of her daughter's death out of her mind. It haunted her day and night.

Whenever William could, he continued to study Greek and Latin and read as many books as he could find. One that he found particularly helpful was called *Help to Zion's Travellers: being an attempt to remove several stumbling blocks out of the way relating to doctrinal, experimental and practical religion.* (Books with long titles sold well in those days!) As he read and reread the book, William became convinced he should be baptized as an adult. He had been baptized as a baby in the Church of St. James the Great, but he wanted baptism to be his own choice and not just his parents' decision for him. On October 5, 1783, William Carey was baptized in the River Nene in Northamptonshire. It was a brisk fall morning when the Reverend John Ryland baptized William and wrote in his journal, "This day baptized a poor journeyman shoemaker." John Ryland had no idea he'd just baptized the man who was to become one of the most famous missionaries the world would know.

Three months after the baptism, Thomas Old, William's employer and brother-in-law, died. William took over his shoemaking business along with the responsibility of supporting Mrs. Old and her four children. William didn't have to do this, but he had a soft heart and felt sorry for them. If William's life had been a struggle up until then, it now became all but impossible. The British had lost the American Revolutionary War, and everyone in England was suffering financially as a result. It was not a good time to start out in business, especially with as little practical experience as William had.

Somehow twenty-three-year-old William had to make enough money to support Mrs. Old, the four Old children, and Dolly. On top of this, he was still trying to study the Bible and preach at struggling dissenter churches. It was a load many young men would have buckled under, but not William.

The winter of 1784 was one of the coldest ever recorded in England. For nine weeks, frost lay heavy on the ground all day long. William nearly froze to death delivering the shoes he had made. Somehow they all made it through, and the next winter was slightly easier. William plodded on, working, studying, and trying to cheer Dolly up, not knowing whether or how things would ever improve for him.

Finally, in 1785, nearly a year after Thomas Old had died, William's circumstances began to change.

William's sister-in-law remarried, releasing William from the burden of taking care of her and her children. Then a tiny Baptist church in Moulton, nine miles to the north, invited William Carey to be their preacher. The church could not afford to offer William much—only fifteen pounds a year for his salary and a meetinghouse that was falling down. Financially, William would not be any better off than he had been making shoes, but this change in profession was a step in the direction William wanted to go. In addition, William would now have time to study the Bible and learn languages without interruption.

With all the enthusiasm of a new minister, William set about rebuilding a congregation that had dwindled to almost nothing in the ten years since the last minister had left. Because the old schoolteacher had left Moulton, William was also able to teach school, which added some extra money to the family income.

While William enjoyed being with the local children, he found it difficult being the schoolmaster. He was not nearly strict enough, and often he smiled at the children's tricks instead of punishing the children as he was supposed to.

William's favorite subject to teach was geography, and William tried hard to interest the children in the world beyond England. This was a difficult task, since none of the children had ever been more than a cart ride away from home. To attract their attention, William drew a large map of the world.

He glued many pieces of paper together and began the painstaking task of copying the continents of the world onto them. To guide him, he used one book in particular, a book about Captain James Cook's explorations. Cook had been killed six years before by natives in the Sandwich Islands (now called Hawaii). Before that, however, he had made three voyages of discovery into the Pacific Ocean. On these voyages, he had mapped new islands and coastlines from Antarctica to Alaska.

Next to each of the continents and islands on his map, William wrote notes about what was known of them. Next to what is now called Australia he wrote: "New Holland 12,000,000 pagans." Next to Easter Island was written: "People thieves. Large statues. No wood. Plantains, yams, potatoes, sugar cane, grown." Next to China was written: "The Chinese are middle-sized with broad faces. Their eyes are black and small, noses blunt, high cheekbones, large lips. Emperors and princes wear yellow. Some mandarins wear black, some red. Common people wear blue. White is for mourning." Next to India was recorded: "Indostan. 110,000,000 Mahamodans, pagans, Brahmins, Sitris, Beise, and Sudders. Rice, pomegranates, oranges, etc. Banyan roots, yams, radishes. 8,000,000 Indians are pagans, vigilant, cruel, warlike."

William Carey was often more moved by the geography lessons than were his young students. Sometimes when he pointed to his map, he would have to stop and take a deep breath before going on. He so much wanted to be out sharing the gospel message with all the different races named on the map. Even though the figures on his map were not accurate, they gave William many restless nights wondering what it would be like to live in a place where the name of Jesus Christ had never been spoken.

William's career as a schoolteacher did not last long. The old schoolteacher came back to Moulton, and overnight, all of William's students reenrolled at his school. This left William with not enough money to feed his wife and their new baby, Felix. William went back to what he knew best—shoemaking. This time, he didn't take on his own business. Instead, he worked under contract to Mr. Gotch, a shoemaker who supplied shoes for the Royal Army and Navy. This meant that William had to make the eleven-mile round trip to Kettering once a week to deliver his batch of new boots and shoes and pick up leather to make more. For all this work, William was paid five shillings a week, which along with the money from being a Baptist minister, was barely enough to buy food for his family.

Up until this time, William was not an ordained (official) Baptist minister. His congregation urged him to become one. After passing a number of exams and preaching in front of many important Baptist ministers of the day, William Carey became an ordained Baptist minister on May 3, 1787. He was twenty-six years old.

Three ministers conducted the ordination service: John Sutcliff, John Ryland (who had baptized William), and Andrew Fuller. It was the first time the three men and William had met together, but it would not be the last. All four of them were destined to remain linked for the rest of their lives.

One of the advantages of being an ordained minister was that William was now able to attend the meetings of the Ministers' Fraternal of the Northampton Association, where he got to listen to the views of many older, well-educated ministers. At the first few meetings, William was too shy to say anything, but he couldn't stay out of such lively discussions for long! He soon found out, however, that many of the other ministers had very different views from his own and did not want a young, upstart minister challenging them.

Chapter 5

# A Miserable Enthusiast

William sat nervously gathering his thoughts during a lull in the conversation at a meeting of the Ministers' Fraternal. One of the older ministers, the Reverend Ryland Sr. (father of William's friend, John Ryland), suggested that perhaps one of the younger members might have a new topic for conversation. All eyes seemed to turn to William, who knew what he wanted to say but just didn't know how to say it the right way. The subject had to do with missions. The more William had read the Bible, the more convinced he had become that God expected Christians to share the gospel message with others, even people far across the ocean in newly discovered lands. This meant that churches in England had an obligation to send out missionaries to these newly discovered places.

This was not a popular view in 1787. Most ministers believed that Jesus had given the task of sharing the gospel message to his twelve disciples and that when they died, so did the job itself. Now no one was required to share his or her faith, especially not in dangerous, unknown regions. Many Christians went so far as to say that if God wanted the heathen in other lands to hear the gospel message, He could tell them Himself without any help from human beings. After all, He was all powerful, wasn't He?

"Reverend Carey, have you come up with a topic yet?" asked the Reverend Ryland Sr.

"Yes," said William, adjusting his wig while still trying to get his thoughts in order. Then he stammered on. "I would like to discuss the idea that when Jesus Christ gave the command to His disciples to preach the gospel to the ends of the earth, He meant it to include, not just His disciples who were alive at that time, but all who would follow Him from then on."

The Reverend Ryland Sr. shot William an angry look and cleared his throat. "Here we have an example of a young man who knows nothing about the plan of God," he said matter-of-factly. "The Almighty does not need a man to speak for Him. He will enlighten the heathen in His own way, when He sees fit. It is not our place to interfere with this process." He glared at William and pointed a finger in his direction for effect before continuing. "And you, young man, are a miserable enthusiast for suggesting otherwise."

With that, the discussion was over. William sat silently thinking about what had been said. Was he really a miserable enthusiast, meddling in things he knew nothing about? Was the Reverend Ryland Sr. right? Should he give up his goal of sharing the gospel message with the heathen? He would have to give the whole subject some more serious thought.

The Reverend Ryland Sr.'s remarks were intended to stop William from considering a Christian's role in evangelizing the world. Surprisingly, though, they encouraged him. The more William thought about the arguments that had been put forward, the more he studied to see who was right. As he studied, he took careful notes. Before long, the notes turned into an essay, which turned into the manuscript for a book.

William found the extra time needed to work on his manuscript from an unlikely source. Mr. Gotch, the man for whom he made shoes under contract, was a member of Andrew Fuller's church in Kettering. The Reverend Fuller had told Mr. Gotch what a fine minister William Carey was becoming. Mr. Gotch began to think that the shoemaker he had contracted to work for him was wasting his talents, so he wrote a letter to William Carey in which he said:

> I do not intend you should spoil anymore of my leather, but you may proceed as fast as you can with your Latin, Greek, and Hebrew, and I will allow you from my own private purse ten shillings a week.

What a surprise awaited William as he opened the letter! From his savings, Mr. Gotch was going to pay him the same amount he had earned making shoes, only now he would be earning the money by studying to become a better minister. William kept on writing and studying, teaching himself Hebrew and Dutch to add to his Latin and Greek. He couldn't have been happier.

Things at home were also going well. Felix now had two little brothers, William Jr. and Peter, who was named after William's favorite uncle. Most of the time, Dolly was fine as well, though sometimes she sat and stared blankly at the walls. She would also cry easily and sometimes forget to take care of the children. This worried William, but there wasn't much he could do about it. His mother had died in 1787, the year before William Jr. was born, and now William had no one to turn to for help.

Although he had the manuscript for his book tucked safely in a leather satchel under his bed, William could not afford to get it published. Ten pounds, the amount needed, was a seventh of his yearly income, and he did not have that kind of money to spare. Besides, he couldn't be sure that anyone would buy a copy of it if it were published. Indeed, if a lot of other people thought the same way as the Reverend Ryland Sr., William could well be run out of town for publishing his manuscript!

Seventeen eighty-nine saw another change for William, who was invited to become the pastor of a slightly larger but more troubled Baptist church in Leicester. William accepted the invitation to pastor the church, even though it meant moving into the smallest cottage he had ever lived in. With three noisy little boys and his wife expecting another baby, it wasn't easy fitting into the cottage, but they all did the best they could. William's salary at the new church was the same small amount it had been in Moulton.

With his growing family, William once again had to think of a way to earn extra money. He decided to try schoolteaching again. While this was not his favorite thing to do, there was no school in Leicester at the time, and he felt sure he could attract enough students to make it worthwhile.

Of course, teaching school made William busier than ever. He taught school from nine in the morning until five in the afternoon. To fit everything in, he made himself a strict schedule for his evenings. The schedule, which he stuck to, was as follows:

MONDAY NIGHT: Study foreign languages and translate something
TUESDAY NIGHT: Study science, history, and composition
WEDNESDAY NIGHT: Preach at church
THURSDAY NIGHT: Visit friends and church members
FRIDAY NIGHT AND ALL DAY SATURDAY: Prepare sermon
SUNDAY: Preaching

Added to this were William's responsibilities as secretary of the Committee of Dissenters, which involved preaching in nearby towns and attending ministerial meetings. All in all, William Carey was a very busy man!

The next Carey baby was a girl, whom they named Lucy. Sometimes William felt sad as he held her and watched her. She reminded him so much of Ann, his first baby daughter, who had died. Tragically, when Lucy was eighteen months old, she too became ill and died. While William was deeply upset by her death, Dolly was thrown more deeply into depression. It took many weeks before she could be coaxed back into family activities. Thankfully, Dolly's younger sister, Kitty, stepped in to help William with the boys.

Despite the family tragedy and his exhaustingly busy schedule, William always had in the back of his mind the thought of telling people in foreign countries about the gospel message. He kept improving his manuscript until finally it was finished. It even had a name—*An enquiry into the obligations of Christians to use means for the conversion of the heathen in which the religious state of the different nations of the world, the success of former undertakings, and the practicability of further undertakings are considered.* It was a very long title, even for those days when long book titles were fashionable. When the manuscript was finally published, most people just called it *Enquiry*.

The book had five chapters. The first dealt with whether Christians in England had an obligation and responsibility to tell people in other lands about the gospel. The second chapter covered all the missionary work that had gone on since the days of Jesus. This chapter had required a lot of research and included a history of the world. The third chapter was a survey of everything that English people knew about the rest of the world. William had spent many hours putting together twenty-three pages of tables about different countries. Each table showed the name of the country or island, its length and breadth, its estimated population, and its religions customs and beliefs. William had begun the basic research for this chapter eight years before, when he'd drawn the map of the world for the schoolhouse in Moulton. By the time he had finished his research, William Carey probably knew more about world geography than anyone else in England. In fact, his book contained more geography, history, and religion than had previously been put into any other single book.

The fourth chapter in William's book was on ways in which Christians could preach the gospel message in foreign lands. It outlined some of the dangers and difficulties a missionary would face and explained the best way to travel to foreign places and how to avoid being killed by heathen people once the missionary arrived. It also covered what foods were safe to eat and how to find a place to live, as well as how to quickly learn a foreign language. William read many books in the course of preparing this chapter, though he had a lot of firsthand knowledge to share about learning foreign languages.

The fifth and final chapter was about how to raise the money needed to go as a missionary to another country.

For its time, *Enquiry* was the most well researched Christian paper ever written, and William Carey wanted desperately to get it published. The question was, How?

In 1791, soon after completing work on the final version of his manuscript, William was attending a ministers' meeting in the city of Birmingham, where he was introduced to a young man named Tom Potts. Tom had been to America, and William wanted to hear all about his trip. William became very interested in Tom's descriptions of the horrible slave trade Tom had seen while in America. Soon the two men were discussing all sorts of things, and William began to talk about the need for missionaries.

"You should write this down!" exclaimed Tom Potts after hearing William's reasons why missionaries were needed in foreign lands. "Every Christian needs to hear the argument for missions as clearly as you have just told it to me."

"As a matter of fact, it is all written down," said William shyly.

"Then tell me where I can buy a copy of your book. What is it called?" asked Tom Potts eagerly.

William admitted the book was not yet published, because of lack of funds.

"The message must get out!" Tom Potts exclaimed. "I would count it an honor to pay for the book to be published myself."

True to his word, Tom Potts paid for the first printing of *Enquiry,* which was published on May 12, 1792, and sold for one shilling and sixpence.

Three weeks after the book was published, William was scheduled to speak at a Baptist ministers' meeting. As always, he spoke about the need for missionaries, but this time something was different. Many of his fellow ministers had already read his book and were beginning to understand what he had been telling them for so long. William Carey finished his speech with two phrases that would ring around the world for more than a century after his death: "Expect great things from God. Attempt great things for God."

At last, several of William's fellow ministers were convinced it was time to attempt something for God! On October 2, 1792, a group of twelve ministers met to make plans. Among them were William's friends John Ryland, Andrew Fuller, and John Sutcliff. The men were all ministers of small churches filled with poor farmers and laborers. Some received enough money from their pastoral duties to support their families, while others, like William, had to take on a second job. All of them wanted to do something to further the cause of missions, but what? In the end, they decided to start a society, which they named the Particular Baptist Society for Propagating the Gospel. Each one in the group promised to give as much money as he could to the new society. When all the pledges were added up, they totaled thirteen pounds. William pledged to give all the money he made from his book. For William, something far greater than the money had happened at the meeting. Finally, after years of preaching about the need for missionaries, William's book had convinced a group of men to take the call seriously. William could hardly wait to see what would happen next.

Many questions were raised at the first official meeting of the Particular Baptist Society for Propagating the Gospel. What qualifications should a missionary have? Did anyone know a person who was qualified and willing to be sent out as a missionary? Where was a good place to send a missionary? What should he do when he got there? Should a missionary have a job there? Should he take his family with him? Should he travel back to England to report on his progress? After all, there had never been an English missionary society before, so there was no pattern to follow.

Obviously, a lot of things had to be thought through before the first missionary could be sent out. As the ministers dealt with all these details, an unspoken question hung in the air: Who would be the first missionary?

Chapter 6

# I Will Go

William Carey turned the envelope over in his hands. He squinted to read the tiny handwriting on it. It was from a Dr. John Thomas, and it was postmarked London. As he slit the envelope open, William tried to think of any connection he had with someone in London. He had never been there himself and couldn't think of anyone he knew there.

William pulled out the letter and began to read. As he read, he got more and more excited. Dr. Thomas had just spent four years in the Bengal region of India. He had originally gone to India as a ship's doctor for the East India Company. While in Calcutta, he had become a Christian, and soon after that he was so overcome with both the spiritual and medical needs of the Indian people that he left his ship and stayed on to work among the people. He had made friends with several English Christians there who had given him money to keep on doing what he was doing. But finally the money had run out, and Dr. Thomas had returned to England to raise more so that he could return to the Bengal region. When he arrived in London, a friend had told him about William Carey and the new missionary society.

*Was it possible that God had sent them their very first missionary so soon?* William wondered as he read. By the time he had finished the letter, he could hardly wait for the next meeting of the missionary society committee to share its contents with the others.

The members of the committee were as impressed with the letter as William had been. Andrew Fuller was given the job of writing to Dr. Thomas and inviting him to attend their next committee meeting in Kettering. The meeting was to be held on January 10, 1793.

Dr. Thomas, who had accepted the invitation, was late, so the meeting started without him. Finally, as the meeting was drawing to a close, there was a knock on the door. William rushed to answer it, wanting to be the first one to greet a real missionary. He shook Dr. Thomas's hand heartily, noting that the doctor looked only about five years older than himself and was a good six inches taller.

Within minutes, William felt as if he and Dr. Thomas were old friends. Dr. Thomas was as passionate about sharing the gospel message with the heathen as William was. The evening sped by.

William, who had written the longest and most researched missionary book of its time, had many questions to ask this real missionary. How much money did it take to keep a family in India? Did Dr. Thomas speak the Bengali language? Did he have some of the language written down so that they could see what it looked like? How many Indians could understand English? What Christian literature was already published in their native languages? How many converts had Dr. Thomas made? How much would it cost to build a humble mud and straw cottage in India? The questions went on and on, and with each answer, William became more excited and more inspired.

Finally, Dr. Thomas pulled a letter from his pocket and read a portion of it. It was from three high-ranking Brahmins (members of India's scholar caste) to whom he had been preaching. The Brahmins had written: "Have compassion on us and send us preachers, and such as will do translation work."

As William heard these words, he felt like his heart would burst. He knew that God had given him a gift for understanding languages quickly, and here were heathen people begging for someone to translate the Bible for them. At that moment, William Carey knew he must go to India.

After putting the letter back in his pocket, Dr. Thomas continued, his voice raised with excitement. "An Englishman should not have any difficulty finding a suitable job within three months of arriving. A man can meet his own expenses and the expenses of his family and still have some left over to use in preaching."

This was what William had been waiting to hear. In his book, *Enquiry,* he had suggested that missionary societies should pay for the missionaries' passage to a foreign land as well as their setup costs when they arrived. As quickly as possible, however, the missionaries should find jobs and become able to support themselves. Now a real missionary was standing in front of him suggesting that this approach was possible in India.

"What is it you desire of us?" Andrew Fuller finally asked Dr. Thomas.

"If you will pay the way for me, my wife, and my daughter and meet our expenses for the first year, I will go back to Bengal and continue the work I began."

Every head in the room nodded.

"And one more thing," Dr. Thomas added. "If a suitable companion could be found to go with me, together we could do a lot more than I could alone."

William Carey could feel his heart beating loudly in his chest. He was the suitable companion; he knew it. He stood firmly to his feet. "I will go," he announced.

All eyes turned to him.

"I will go," he repeated.

"Yes. Go! There is a gold mine of souls to be dug for in India," said Andrew Fuller, rushing over to shake his friend's hand.

"I will go down the mine," William replied seriously, "if you will all hold the ropes for me."

It was a solemn moment. William looked carefully from Andrew Fuller to John Sutcliff and then to John Ryland. Each man knew exactly what William meant. If he was to go to India, he would have to be able to count on them 100 percent to support him. The three men gathered around William and made him a promise. "I pledge to support you, no matter what happens, until the day I die," each one repeated in turn. Right then and there, the course for the rest of William Carey's life was set. He knew there would be no turning back.

William and Dr. Thomas talked far into the night. By the time they parted ways the following morning, their plans were firm. They would leave for India around April 1, in about three months. This would give them time to raise the money they needed. Dr. Thomas explained to William that it would take about five months to get to India, and if they didn't start the journey before mid-May, the winds would be blowing in the wrong direction.

As William hiked back through the country lanes to his home in Leicester, he began wondering what other people would think of his decision. Would they understand? What would Dolly say? She had never been more than thirty miles from the cottage where she was born. Neither had William, for that matter, but unlike him, Dolly had no spirit for adventure. Everything made her nervous. And then there was the matter of her latest pregnancy.

Dolly Carey was expecting another baby. It was due in May, which William knew meant that the child would be born at sea. Thank goodness, Dr. and Mrs. Thomas would be on board to help if anything went wrong.

Then there was his father. What would he say? He was still a clerk in the Church of England, and William didn't think his father would be one bit impressed with what he was about to do. And his congregation. How would the members of the Harvey Lane Baptist Church react when they heard the news? Under William's leadership, the church had left its troubled past behind and was growing rapidly. In fact, the church had just built a new gallery to provide extra seating for all the people who had joined the church.

As William walked, he prayed about these things. He knew beyond a doubt that God had called him to go halfway around the world to India. He just hoped that the people he loved most in the world would understand.

"What a wild idea!" screamed Dolly when her husband announced the news. "How can you think of me going to India when I have a baby on the way? God have mercy, is there not enough for you to do in England? And think of the boys. Felix, William, Peter, all those native diseases. I've buried two children, and it would be the death of me to lose another." Tears of despair flowed down her cheeks, but she was not finished. "And the voyage, in a little boat out on that great big ocean. I couldn't do it. I just couldn't do it. It's cruel of you to even suggest it."

William reached out to take her hand. Although she had never seen the ocean, he knew how much she feared it.

"We must leave it in God's hands," he said soothingly.

"In God's hands, indeed!" his wife snapped back angrily, pulling her hand away. "I will not go, and that's final. If you want to leave us all behind, you can go alone. That's all I have to say about it."

William Carey sighed deeply. He knew from experience that it would be almost impossible to change his wife's mind. Still, it was not too unusual for eighteenth-century men to leave their wives and families for long periods. Some men went to war, others searched for gold, and men like Captain Cook were away for years at a time exploring. Surely, going to share the gospel message with those who had never heard it before was a more noble reason to go alone than any of these other reasons, William comforted himself.

Next, it was time to tell his father of his plans. The following Saturday, William sat down and wrote him the following letter:

Leicester, January 17, 1793

Dear and honored father,

The importance of spending our time for God alone is the principal theme of the gospel. I beseech you, brethren, says Paul, by the mercies of God, that ye present your bodies a living sacrifice, holy and acceptable, which is your reasonable service. To be devoted like a sacrifice to holy uses is the great business of a Christian....

I consider myself as devoted to the service of God alone and now I am to realize my professions. I am appointed to go to Bengal in the East Indies, a missionary to the Hindoos [*sic*].... I have many sacrifices to make, I must part with a beloved family and a number of most affectionate friends...but I have set my hand to the plough.

I remain your dutiful son,
W. Carey

It was just as well William sent the letter rather than deliver the news in person. His sister Polly later told him that their father had been very angry when he read the letter and had yelled, "Has William gone mad? How can a person who has to keep out of the midday sun in England hope to survive in the tropics? And what about his wife and children?" Edmund Carey no doubt was also thinking that if William went through with his scheme, he may never see his son again. He was right.

The following Sunday, William decided it was time to tell his congregation of his plans. After all, he told himself, if he did not tell them soon, someone else would, since news was getting around. It was with a heavy heart that William broke the news to his congregation. The next day he wrote in his journal, "Never did I see such sorrow manifested as reigned through our place of worship last Lord's day."

Over the next several weeks, though, the church came to accept the news. The members of the congregation had been praying for several years that God would send missionaries to the heathen, and now they understood that their church was being asked to make the first sacrifice. While they were losing a pastor they loved very much, they were gaining a missionary. Soon they began to get excited about the whole venture.

Dolly Carey, however, did not change her position at all. William's two friends, John Sutcliff and Andrew Fuller, both walked to Leicester to beg her to reconsider, but she would not. Finally, William had to face the fact that he would be going to India without her. His new plan was to set up a mission base somewhere in the Bengal region, and when he had a nice house and garden, he would come back for his family. He thought this would take him three or four years to accomplish. He was hopeful that by then, Dolly would have adjusted to the idea of going to India. Still, the thought of leaving his family behind was an awful one for William. Finally, he persuaded Dolly to let him take eight-year-old Felix along. That way he would have at least one family member with him.

The next question was what to do with Dolly Carey, the other two boys, and the new baby during the years William would be away. Since William would no longer be the pastor of the church, Dolly would not be able to continue living in the church manse, and she had no way of supporting herself. The missionary society agreed to support her, and Dolly decided to move in with her sister Kitty, who lived in Piddington.

While it was generous of the society to offer to look after William's family while he was gone, in reality it didn't have the money to do it. The entire society had only eighty-eight pounds in the bank.

On top of supporting Dolly and the family, the society had to have money to pay for William, Felix, and the three members of the Thomas family to get to India and establish themselves. Altogether, the society needed over five hundred fifty pounds, a huge amount at that time. William felt the only way to raise that kind of money was to involve every Baptist church in England. But how could they do that?

Finally, it was decided that William, Dr. Thomas, and Andrew Fuller would spend several weeks on a speaking tour of the country trying to convince people of the need for missionaries. The men would sell copies of *Enquiry* and ask their audiences to pledge money to the cause. It was something that had never been done before, and no one was sure whether it would work. The truth was, sometimes it did and sometimes it didn't. In Birmingham, the speakers received a warm welcome and the promise of two hundred pounds to help their cause.

In the town of Bath, it was a different story. The offering in Bath netted exactly one penny! Dr. Thomas couldn't believe that the people of Bath were so uncaring about missions. At the end of the meeting, he stood to his feet and announced, "Thank you for coming to listen to us. Your financial contribution of one penny will be gratefully recorded in the mission society's ledger, alongside the gifts of other towns."

A murmur rolled through the crowd. The people were embarrassed. How could they allow other towns to know they had given only a penny to the new missionaries? Someone grabbed the offering basket and sent it around for a second offering. This time there was a much more generous twenty-pound pledged, and the one penny from Bath was never recorded in the ledger.

In London, none of the Baptist churches would support them. The ministers there held many meetings to discuss the issue, but in the end, they decided it was God's job to reach the heathen, not theirs. Besides, there was a lot of work to be done in England, and it seemed ridiculous to them that someone would want to make such a dangerous journey just to share the gospel message.

Despite the setback in London, William Carey enjoyed his trip throughout England. On horseback and on foot, he and his companions traveled several hundred miles. Along the way, William saw for the first time things he'd only read or heard about. He stood on the seashore and looked out across the frigid North Sea. He had tried to imagine all his life what the sea must be like, and now he was seeing it. He went to London and crossed the River Thames and saw the Tower of London. The things he saw were more amazing than he'd imagined. But more than all these sights, William enjoyed the trip because it gave him the opportunity to share in person with thousands of people, both in large churches and in small cottages, his ideas about the need for missionaries.

At a meeting in Hull, William met a young man who greatly impressed him by the name of William Ward. After the meeting was over, William Ward stayed behind to talk to William Carey. He told how he was a printer who worked for the local newspaper. William's mind whirled as he heard this. He thought of Dr. Thomas's letter from the Brahmins about the need for translation work, and his eyes lit up. "If God blesses us, we will be needing someone like you in India to help us print the Scriptures. I hope you will consider joining us in three or four years," he told William Ward.

The two men shook hands, and William Carey left for his next meeting, but the young printer never forgot the conversation. He and William Carey were destined to meet again.

After several weeks of traveling throughout England, the trio had raised enough money to pay for five passages to India, outfit the men, and keep

Dolly Carey and the boys for one year. There was even some money left over to buy a trunkful of metal goods to sell when they arrived in India.

Dr. Thomas had convinced William and the rest of the committee that the money raised from the sale of the metal goods would be enough to keep them all for at least a year. However, during the time they had been out raising the money for their voyage, two important events had occurred. The first event had to do with France. The French had declared war on England and Holland again. This meant that the seas around Great Britain were filled with French pirate ships, or privateers, as they were called. With the permission of the French government, these ships waited to attack and prey on British ships leaving port. Many captains feared for their lives as they set out from English ports. It was a dangerous time to be flying the English flag on the open sea.

The second event was even more important because it meant that even if the ship carrying William and the Thomases got safely past the privateers and made it to India, when they got there they would not be welcome. In 1600, Queen Elizabeth I had given a group of wealthy businessmen a charter to establish a company that would be the exclusive English agency for trade with India. The company was called the East India Company, and it was soon the world leader in the export of calico, indigo dye, cotton, silk, spices, and tea. In 1793, a bill to extend the East India Company's charter was before the British Parliament. However, a growing number of people in England believed that the British had an obligation to help civilize the native peoples in far-off lands. These people began asking Parliament to allow teachers and even missionaries to go to India to aid in the process.

Up to this point, as part of its charter, the East India Company had the authority to say who would be issued permits to enter India and who would not, and it issued permits only to merchants and government officials. And that was how the company wanted things to stay. The last thing it needed was teachers and missionaries meddling in Indian affairs. Who knew what might happen if the Indian people started hearing about such things as freedom and independence! It was in the best interests of the East India Company to keep the local people ignorant of such ideas. That way, the people would keep working hard and not ask questions. Thus, the powerful businessmen who ran the East India Company set about persuading Parliament not to listen to the arguments of those who wanted to "meddle" in Indian affairs, and instead pass a bill extending the company's charter unchanged. That is precisely what Parliament did.

This was bad news for the first ever Baptist missionaries, who knew there was no way they would be granted a permit to enter India; and if they entered illegally, they could be fined and put in jail. The problem bothered William and Dr. Thomas for some time. What were they to do? Then Dr.

Thomas came up with an idea. He had been a ship's doctor aboard the *Earl of Oxford,* and he was still good friends with the ship's captain. Dr. Thomas persuaded Captain White to take the group to India without a permit. Once they got there, they would have to find some way to stay.

William was not happy with the plan. Yet he had to admit that there seemed no other way around the East India Company's rules. He decided to seek the advice of a man he'd heard a lot about, the Reverend John Newton. Newton had been the captain of a slave ship before becoming a Christian and was now a well-known minister.

William explained the situation to John Newton and asked what he should do if the authorities in India wouldn't let him land without a permit. The Reverend Newton answered, "Then conclude that your God has nothing there for you to accomplish. But if He has, no power on earth can hinder you."

William was very encouraged by these words. "No power on earth can hinder you," he would repeat often to himself. If God wanted him to get to India, no power on earth was going to stop him!

On April 4, 1793, just three months after their first meeting, William Carey, his son Felix, and Dr. and Mrs. Thomas and their four-year-old daughter, Eliza, stood side by side on the deck of the *Earl of Oxford* as she sailed from London down the River Thames and out into the North Sea. At thirty-one years of age, William Carey was finally on his way to the mission field—or so he had every reason to believe!

Chapter 7

# Bad News, Good News

"It's a pity we cannot be on our way directly," sighed Captain White. The *Earl of Oxford* had left the safety of the River Thames an hour before and was now sailing in the open waters of the North Sea. William and Dr. Thomas stood next to the captain on the aft deck. "With the French at war with us, it's just too dangerous," he continued. "I've seen their ships on the horizon, and I fear we would never make it out into the Atlantic Ocean."

William nodded. He'd seen the sails of the French privateers on the horizon. The ships seemed to sit there daring British ships to come within their reach.

"We will be much better off sailing in a convoy. I've ordered the first mate to hug the coast until we get to the Isle of Wight. We'll anchor off Portsmouth until there are enough other ships to run the gauntlet."

"How long will that be?" Dr. Thomas nervously asked Captain White.

"It all depends on what other ships are already in port. I would hope it won't be more than a day or two, a week at the most."

"A week!" echoed Dr. Thomas.

William frowned. His companion seemed unusually worried about the loss of a few days.

When the ship arrived off the Isle of Wight, the news was not encouraging. A convoy had left the day before, and it could be a month or more before enough ships gathered to form another one.

Captain White suggested that the group would be much more comfortable in the town of Portsmouth. William went ashore and found a cheap boardinghouse where they could all stay while they waited for the other ships to gather. The group left most of their luggage on board, taking only a few clothes with them.

William wrote to Dolly explaining the delay and inquiring whether the baby had been born yet. In the letter he wrote:

> If I had all the world, I would freely give it all to have you and my dear children with me; but the sense of duty is so strong as to overpower all other considerations; I could not turn back without guilt on my soul.... Let me know the dear little child's name—I am, forever, your faithful and affectionate husband,
>
> William Carey

While William busied himself teaching Felix, writing letters, and visiting local churches, he noticed that Dr. Thomas had begun acting very strangely. Whenever there was a knock at the door, Dr. Thomas would hurry into the back room and peer out at the visitor through a crack in the wall. He would also ask the landlord three or four times a day whether there was any mail for him. When he did receive a letter, he seemed afraid to open it.

William wondered what was going on. Why was his partner acting like this? He didn't have to wait long to find out. During the third week of their stay in Portsmouth, Dr. Thomas insisted he had to go to London on some urgent business. While he was gone, the others had a visitor, one Dr. Thomas had every right to be worried about. It was a merchant from Brighton who had come to collect the hundred pounds he claimed Dr. Thomas owed him.

William was shocked. Dr. Thomas had told him he had a few overdue bills to pay off, but surely he hadn't intended leaving England still owing a hundred pounds. It must have been a mistake.

William waited for the doctor to arrive back from London to explain the situation. But Dr. Thomas could not. It was all true. Dr. Thomas did owe the merchant from Brighton a hundred pounds, and worse, he had other debts that together totaled five hundred pounds. William was worried. If only the *Earl of Oxford* had left a day earlier and caught the departing convoy, he wouldn't have had to know about any of this. Now the situation weighed heavily on his mind. Was it right to go to India with a missionary partner who was in so much debt?

The question seemed to be answered for him in a most depressing way. Three days later, a note arrived from Captain White. The captain had received an anonymous letter saying that the East India Company knew he had male passengers on board who were trying to enter India without a permit and that he would lose his captain's license if he took the men any farther.

William showed the note to Dr. Thomas. "It looks as if we cannot sail after all," he sighed.

"I think this is the work of one of my creditors," replied Dr. Thomas. "I will go back to London to see what can be done."

It was too late, however. When William went to the waterfront with Felix, Mrs. Thomas, and Eliza, the *Earl of Oxford* was moored alongside the dock where Captain White had already unloaded their baggage. Sailors were scurrying up the rigging, and it was obvious the ship was preparing to set sail. William begged Captain White to reconsider, but he would not. It was simply not worth his career to take a couple of missionaries on board. However, he did agree to take Mrs. Thomas and Eliza with him, since the note specifically mentioned only men.

An hour later, William and Felix, surrounded by wooden crates and leather trunks, watched the *Earl of Oxford* hoist her sails. Although William felt sad that he was not aboard, it was a magnificent sight to see. There were six sailing ships headed together out into the English Channel on a fresh spring afternoon. Mrs. Thomas and Eliza waved at them from the stern of the *Earl of Oxford.*

As the ships sailed toward the horizon, William wondered what would happen now. Had he done the right thing allowing Mrs. Thomas and Eliza to go on alone? What if Dr. Thomas never made it to India? William turned his back on the ships and picked up one of the smaller crates lying beside him on the dock. There were more questions than answers, but for now he had to store their baggage and find Dr. Thomas and tell him what had happened.

William hired a small cart to take their belongings back to the boardinghouse. Then he and Felix boarded a coach for London. Besides finding Dr. Thomas, William knew he had to write a letter to Andrew Fuller and the missionary society committee. The trouble was, he wasn't sure what to say in the letter.

Once in London, William and Felix went straight to the house where Dr. Thomas was staying to break the news to him. The doctor apologized many times for what had happened and vowed to find another way to get them to India. William wondered about going to the East India Company and begging for entry permits, but he knew his chances of getting them were almost impossible. Then he thought about traveling overland from Holland to Calcutta, India, but that would be a very long and dangerous journey. Finally, Dr. Thomas had an idea, though he would not say what it was. Instead, he grabbed his hat and coat and raced out the door. He returned an hour later, out of breath but waving a piece of paper. "I think I'm onto something here," he said, thrusting the paper at William. The paper read: "A Danish East Indiaman, no. 10 Cannon St."

"It's the address of a Danish seaman," Dr. Thomas went on. "I got the address from a pub owner down by the docks. He is waiting for his ship to dock in England on its way from Copenhagen to India. If God is with us, there may be room aboard for three passengers. Come, we must hurry."

William grabbed his hat and coat and followed Dr. Thomas out the door, with Felix trailing along behind. As they hurried along the cobbled streets to Cannon Street, William and Dr. Thomas talked excitedly. A foreign ship going to India would not be under the control of the East India Company, so they would not need permits to travel. Even better, a Danish ship would be headed for the Danish-controlled city of Serampore and not to one of the cities under East India Company control. William could feel hope rising within. Was it possible they had found a legal way to get into India?

When they arrived at number 10 Cannon Street, the news was exciting. The Danish seaman was waiting for his ship, the *Kron Princessa Maria,* which was expected to dock within the next few days at Dover, sixty miles away on the south coast of England. The seaman said that as far as he knew, there were passenger cabins available aboard the ship.

"How much does a passage cost?" William asked.

"One hundred pounds for each adult, fifty pounds for a child, and twenty-five pounds for a servant," replied the Danish seaman, who then gave them the name of the ship's agent in London where passage could be arranged and paid for.

William quickly thanked the man for the information and stepped outside into the early evening. It would cost the three of them two hundred fifty pounds to get to India, but all they had was the one hundred fifty pounds Captain White had refunded to them. What were they to do?

Dr. Thomas was all for William and Felix going on alone, but William would not hear of it. By now he was convinced that Dr. Thomas was a good man and really would try his best to pay back the money he owed. Since they had set out to go to India together, William decided they would just have to find a way to get there together.

They still didn't know what to do when they got back to the house where Dr. Thomas was staying. There on the sidetable in the hallway was a letter addressed to the Reverend William Carey. William picked up the letter, which was written in the clumsy handwriting his wife wrote in since he'd taught her to read and write. He opened it eagerly.

The news was wonderful. He had a new baby son, whom Dolly had named Jabez. William knew that Jabez was Hebrew for "in sorrow," and at that moment, he felt very far away from his beloved wife and children. *What I would not give to see the new baby,* he thought. Then suddenly, he clapped his hands together. "There is time. Yes, there is time," he yelled at Dr. Thomas.

Dr. Thomas looked back at him with wondering eyes.

"Of course, we can do it," said William, pushing his chair back and pacing around the room.

"Do what?" asked the doctor.

"If we take the coach tonight, we will be in Piddington by morning. Maybe God meant this delay so that the baby could be born and my wife would be ready to come with us."

Within half an hour, the two men and Felix had thrown a few items into a leather bag and were rushing off to catch the next coach headed for Northamptonshire. By daybreak, they had been dropped off within a mile of Piddington, where Dolly now lived with her sister Kitty.

Dolly Carey's mouth dropped open when she unlatched the cottage door and found her husband, oldest son, and Dr. Thomas waiting outside. Dolly quickly welcomed them in, and soon William was sitting and holding baby Jabez. He did not waste any time in telling his wife that he'd come back to get her. He begged and pleaded with her, but still she would not change her mind. Yes, the baby was now safely born, she told William, but still there would be many dangers for her and the boys. She would not go with him.

Kitty prepared breakfast for the men while Dolly and William talked. The men ate the meal gratefully, and once they were finished, William knew they must be on their way again. They needed to walk to Northampton to meet with John Ryland, in the hope that he had collected some more money for their passage to India.

William hugged his two sons and new baby good-bye and kissed his wife. This time it seemed harder to leave. With a heavy heart, William set a fast walking pace for Northampton, but the pace did not last. William was simply too upset about leaving his wife and family. He was sure that God had delayed their trip so that they would come with him, but Dolly would not budge. Finally, William sat down by the side of the road and wept.

Dr. Thomas could not bear to see his friend so sad. Something had to be done. "Come on, William, we're going back," he said, gently pulling William to his feet. "It is not right to separate a family like this."

William quietly followed Dr. Thomas as the two men retraced their steps. Soon they were outside the cottage. The door was open, and inside they could see Dolly sitting by the hearth sobbing. When she saw them, she wiped her eyes on her apron and stood up. "What is it?" she asked, her tears replaced by a surprised look.

"It is you, Mrs. Carey," replied Dr. Thomas sternly. "We have come back to give you one more chance. It is not right to break up a family. God has sent William to India, and his family should be with him. Have you considered that you might never see him again? That the boys would grow up without knowing their father? How would you ever forgive yourself if this were the last moment you saw your husband alive?"

Dolly Carey was speechless. She looked from Dr. Thomas to her husband and back again. "But I am too scared to go alone," she finally burst out. "And what about my family? Is it fair that Kitty and I will not see each other again?"

"Perhaps Kitty will agree to come with us," said Dr. Thomas, calmly looking at Dolly's sister.

Kitty turned bright red. "I couldn't—I mean I…" Her sentence trailed off, and she sat down beside her sister and clung to her for support. For a long time, the room was silent except for the little grunting noises Jabez made in his sleep.

Suddenly Kitty stood up. Her whole body was shaking as she spoke. "If it keeps the family together, then I will go." Then she turned to Dolly and said, "We will go together, and I will help you."

William watched as Dolly's eyes grew wider. Then Dolly nodded. "All right. We will go together," she said quietly.

William rushed to his wife and hugged her. Dolly and the rest of their children were going to India after all!

The rest of the day turned into a crazy race to get two women and three children packed and ready for a five-month sea voyage and whatever lay beyond in India. Five-year-old William Jr. and four-year-old Peter scurried in and out of the cottage. Dr.

Thomas stayed behind to help, since he knew what a family would need both on the ship and in India. He collected and packed all their bedding and warm clothes, since they would be headed into midwinter as they sailed into the Southern Hemisphere.

As the day wore on, news traveled quickly around the village. Soon, astonished neighbors were visiting Dolly and Kitty to see for themselves that they were really packing to go to India.

While Dr. Thomas helped with the packing, William set out a second time for Northampton. This time, he sang hymns as he walked. John Ryland was thrilled to hear that the whole family would be going with William to India. However, he had not collected any more money for the group. He did have two hundred pounds of his own in the bank, but it was Saturday, and he would not be able to get the money until ten o'clock Monday morning.

William groaned. The *Kron Princessa Maria* might have come and gone by then. After much discussion, John Ryland came up with a plan. He had several rich friends in London who he felt sure would have two hundred pounds tucked away between them. Hurriedly, John Ryland wrote letters asking his friends to lend the money to William and promising to repay it before the end of the week.

There was no time to lose. William thanked his friend and half walked and half ran back to Piddington. By the time he arrived, the family was packed. Early the next morning, the whole family and Dr. Thomas boarded a stagecoach bound for London.

Dolly peered out the window as the familiar sights that had surrounded her all her life disappeared from view and were replaced with lanes and villages she had never seen before. Kitty reached out and gave her sister's hand a reassuring squeeze as the coach rumbled along.

William, with Peter sitting on his knee, looked out the window, too, but he was not thinking of the scene flashing before him. He was doing math—the same math—over and over. He had one hundred fifty pounds in his pocket from Captain White's refund, and he had two hundred pounds to collect in London. That made a total of three hundred fifty pounds. But there were now four adults sailing to India at one hundred pounds each. That made four hundred pounds, plus four children at fifty pounds each. Altogether their passage to India would cost six hundred pounds, two hundred fifty pounds more than he had!

William took a deep breath as he wondered what to do. How ironic it would be, he thought, if after convincing Dolly to travel to India with him, they could not leave because there wasn't enough money for her passage. Finally, William prayed a silent prayer. "God, You have brought me this far. You have even got Dolly and the children to come. Surely You will show us a way to get to India."

The group arrived in London on Sunday evening. William had no difficulty in finding one of John Ryland's friends who was willing to lend him the two hundred pounds. As soon as he arrived back with the money, Dr. Thomas took it and the refunded one hundred fifty pounds and went to see the ship's agent. Being Dr. Thomas, he had another plan, a plan that he'd discussed with no one but Kitty. Several hours later he returned, waving eight tickets, one for each of them.

"How did you do it?" asked William, with a broad smile.

"I think the agent was impressed with a whole family traveling together. I asked him if Kitty and I might travel as your servants, and he asked me how much money we actually had for the passages. When I said three hundred fifty pounds, he told me India needed missionaries and that a man should not be separated from his family, so if that was all the money we had, then it was enough to get us there. We are bound for India!"

"When does the ship sail?" asked William, after he had examined each of the tickets.

"We must hurry. She sets sail from Dover tomorrow afternoon on the high tide."

William gasped. It was impossible for them to make it on time, and what about the luggage they had left in Portsmouth?

Dr. Thomas reached into his pocket and pulled out some more tickets. "I called on an old friend, and he gave me enough money to buy the rest of you ferry tickets to Dover."

"And what about you?" asked William.

"I intend to leave this very minute for Portsmouth to collect the baggage. If God blesses me, I will meet you in Dover with it tomorrow."

Chapter 8

# A Course to India

Dr. Thomas made it to Dover in time with the baggage, which was now stowed safely below deck. The crew was busy making the ship ready to sail. Sailors in the rigging above were unfurling the mainsail. Others were busily stowing or lashing to the deck barrels and crates of all shapes and sizes. Finally, the captain bellowed the order: "Cast off!"

The fore and aft lines that had held the ship securely against the quay were let go, and the *Kron Princessa Maria* began to drift to sea. William watched as the bustle of people on the quay got smaller and smaller. For the second time in a month, he was setting sail for India, only this time his wife and four sons were standing next to him on the aft deck.

As the ship made its way out into the Straits of Dover, the British frigate *Triton* was waiting. The *Triton* had been hired to escort the *Kron Princessa Maria* through the English Channel and on into the Bay of Biscay. While the Danes were not at war with the French, and therefore were free of the threat of attack, the truth was that the French privateers sometimes got carried away and plundered any ship that was not French.

As the *Triton* sailed in next to them, William watched the chalky white cliffs of Beachy Head fade from view, and with them, the last glimpse he and his family would ever have of their homeland.

In his journal that night, William wrote: "Thursday, June 13, 1793, on board the *Kron Princessa Maria.* This has been a day of gladness to my soul. I was returned that I might take all my family with me and enjoy all the blessings which I had surrendered to God."

William spent the next few days with the oldest three boys—Felix, William Jr., and Peter—exploring from stem to stern the one-hundred-thirty-foot long schooner that would be their home on the journey to India. They explored above deck and below, checking out what was stored in the ship's hold, and climbing around the rigging, being careful not to slip or go too high. They peered over the side of the ship as William explained how the hulls of most modern ships, like the *Kron Princessa Maria,* had a copper sheet over their wooden planks. This meant that the ships could go much faster, even making it to India and back in twelve months!

For William and the boys, the voyage was a great adventure. But not for Dolly and Kitty. The week before they had been happily adjusting to life together in their home village of Piddington, not more than a mile from where they were born. Now they were on a ship, pitching and turning in the open ocean, and far away from the safety of their home. Dolly didn't even like to go up on deck; the vastness of the ocean without a speck of land in sight scared her. And the sound of the crew talking to each other in Danish and Norwegian reminded her that she was leaving the English language behind as well.

Besides Dolly and Kitty, there was one other woman on board, a Black woman who stayed and ate with the crew. She was the first Black person Dolly had ever seen, and the sight of the woman's flashing white eyes frightened her.

Captain Christmas, an Englishman who had taken Danish citizenship, was very kind. Even though the missionaries had not paid nearly as much as the other four passengers aboard (two Frenchmen and two Englishmen), the captain did his best to make the voyage comfortable for William and his family. He gave them the largest cabin, which William wrote was "half the width of the ship with south windows and papered sides [walls]." He even invited them all to eat at the captain's table, where each evening for the first few weeks of the voyage they feasted on three-course dinners that included at least two types of meat and a large dessert. They were eating better food than they had in their entire lives. Instead of wasting away at sea, as Dolly had feared, the family got stronger everyday. Little Jabez got so fat that his father took to calling him his "stout fellow."

Once the ship was safely across the Bay of Biscay and headed out into the Atlantic Ocean, William's life at sea settled into a routine. William held a prayer meeting in his cabin each morning and night, with much of the rest of his day spent learning the Bengali language from Dr. Thomas. Although Dr. Thomas didn't know all the ins and outs of the complicated language, he shared William's passion to see the Bible written down in the various Indian languages. The two men worked together translating the Book of Genesis into Bengali. William's knowledge of Hebrew was a great help in the process. In his spare time, William took notes from the one hundred or so botanical books and magazines he had brought along with him.

As the ship approached the equator, the days got steadily hotter, and as they did so, William made a personal decision. He was leaving England behind him and starting a new life in a foreign country, and no matter what, he wasn't going to begin this new life wearing his hot, scratchy wig! It was time for the wig to go. One morning before the rest of the family was up, William climbed the stairs to the aft deck and flung his wig overboard into the Atlantic Ocean. How good it felt to be rid of it. The breeze blew gently over William's bald head. When Dr. Thomas came up on deck and saw William, he laughed with relief. He said, "Mr. Wilson of Olney [who made the wig for William] is an excellent Christian, but he is one of the worst wigmakers that ever was born!" Both men laughed heartily.

Besides spending time with his family and Dr. Thomas, William became very friendly with Captain Christmas, a well-educated man who delighted in showing William how he plotted their course to India. William had been interested in navigation ever since reading about how Captain Cook had used a Harrison chronometer to plot latitude. William would watch as the captain used his sextant to take readings from the stars at night and the sun during the day. Then from the readings, Captain Christmas would show how he calculated the ship's position on the large map rolled out on the table in the corner of his cabin.

The course the captain had plotted for the *Kron Princessa Maria* took them down the northwest coast of Africa until they caught the northwesterly trade winds. They would use these winds to take them across the Atlantic Ocean almost to South America. Once they reached Trinidad Island off the coast of Rio de Janeiro, Brazil, they would pick up the southeasterly winds, which would take them across the South Atlantic, past the tiny island of Tirstan da Cunha—their most southerly point on the journey—and then due east past the Cape of Good Hope at the southern tip of Africa and on into the Indian Ocean. There the *Kron Princessa Maria* would again pick up the southeasterly winds, which would push her all the way to the equator, not far off the coast of the Dutch East Indies (now Indonesia). There the northwesterly monsoon winds would fill the sails and drive them all the way into the Bay of Bengal and on to Calcutta, which lay at the northern end of the bay.

If everything went according to plan, the whole journey should take about five months. However, the winds were seasonal, and if they arrived too late to catch a trade wind, they would have to wait six months until the winds began blowing in the right direction again.

At the Cape of Good Hope, the ship was scheduled to dock for several days at Cape Town. As they neared the cape, William and Dr. Thomas busied themselves writing letters to mail when they docked. But Captain Christmas was getting anxious. The winds were not as strong as they usually were, and time was running out. They had to make it across the Bay of Bengal before the end of the monsoon season in early October. As a result, the ship did not put in at Cape Town but kept straight on going out into the Indian Ocean. William stuffed the letters to his father and the missionary society committee back into his pouch. He would just have to mail them when he got to India.

Dolly wasn't happy about this. No one had told her she would be aboard ship for five months without once getting off to feel land beneath her feet! It's just as well they didn't stop in Cape Town, however, because had Dolly Carey known what lay ahead, she would have insisted on being left behind there.

All was going well until William was called to perform a funeral service at sea. The Black woman traveling on the ship had become ill and died. She was buried at sea off the Cape of Good Hope. The death and funeral made Dolly even more nervous. Dolly had tried hard not to think of the dangers involved in what the family was doing, but the woman's death brought all her fears flooding back. Dolly clung to the children and hardly let them out of the cabin. She spent her days sitting in the cabin, facing away from the porthole.

Then in the early morning hours of August 26, the *Kron Princessa Maria* ran into a violent storm. Fifty-foot high waves crashed around the little ship, tossing it one way and then the other. Every plank in the hull moaned and creaked. William was jarred awake with the scream of one of the boys being tossed from his bunk by the pitching, rolling ship. He leapt from his bed, trying to steady himself as best he could. He found William Jr. shaking and still on the floor where he had landed. William helped him back into his bunk. Dolly was already awake and clutching Jabez tightly against her. She was crying quietly, and William put his arm around her to comfort her as he stumbled back into bed.

Soon the cabin door flung open, and Kitty staggered in from her cabin next door. Her face was white, and she was trembling as she climbed onto the bed. William tried to comfort them all as they listened to the thunderous waves break against the ship. Above all the noise, they could hear Captain

Christmas on deck frantically barking orders to the crew.

William was wondering what he should do next when Dr. Thomas appeared in the doorway. Dr. Thomas braced his arms and legs against the door frame as the ship rolled violently. "It looks bad," he yelled against the backdrop of crashing waves and the creaking of the hull. "The main and fore topmasts have been washed overboard."

"Stay in your bunks," William instructed his family. "I'm going to see if they need help." He pulled on his shirt and trousers and headed off into the darkness with Dr. Thomas.

The storm raged for two days, during which time William and Dr. Thomas took their turn helping the crew make sure the things stowed on deck stayed lashed down, and cutting free tangled lengths of rigging and broken yardarms that had snapped and swung menacingly in the ferocious wind. Then, as quickly as the storm had come, it was gone, but not before the sails had been shredded to rags and two of the three masts had broken.

It took ten days of feverish work to rig a jury-mast where the main mast had been and patch enough of the torn sails to get the *Kron Princessa Maria* under way again. Although no one was killed during the storm, several days later, the ship's carpenter died as a result of pneumonia he caught during the storm. Once again, William held a funeral service at sea.

Beyond worrying about his own situation, William thought about all the continents and islands they had passed during the voyage. He wondered how many people in those places had never heard the gospel message. William put his thoughts down in a letter to the missionary society committee:

> I hope the Society will go on and increase, and that the multitudes of heathen in the world may hear the glorious words of truth. Africa is but a little way from England; Madagascar but a little way farther; South America, and all the numerous and large islands in the Indian and Chinese Seas, I hope will not be passed over. A large field opens on every side and millions of perishing heathens tormented in this side by idolatry, superstition, and ignorance, and exposed to eternal miseries in the world to come are pleading.

As they headed farther out into the Indian Ocean, the situation aboard the *Kron Princessa Maria* became more desperate with each passing day. There was no more meat or pudding for dinner, not even at the captain's table. The quartermaster had stowed only enough food and water to get from Dover to Cape Town, where normally they would have taken on more supplies. But since they hadn't stopped in Cape Town, the quartermaster was forced to ration what little food was left. They were blessed to have some rain showers along the way, and the water that fell on the ship was carefully collected and stored in barrels on deck.

Finally, in October, the small Danish ship, proudly flying its red flag with a white cross on it, sailed into the Bay of Bengal. They were now only two hundred miles from their destination. But Captain Christmas was worried, and he was right to worry. The last of the monsoon winds had come and gone. Now the wind and current were against them, flowing out of the north. It was going to be a slow and tedious job sailing north toward their destination.

A sailing ship cannot sail directly into a headwind. It has to zigzag, or *tack,* as it is called, backward and forward across the wind, inching its way slowly in the direction of the headwind. William, who was interested in the whole process of navigation and sailing, spent many hours bent over the map with Captain Christmas, charting their progress. He wrote about what he learned in his diary:

> A ship sails within six [compass] points of the wind; that is, if the wind blows from the North, a ship will sail ENE [east northeast] upon one tack, and WNW [west northwest] upon the other; if our course is North, we must therefore go ENE for a considerable way, then WNW; and if the wind shifts a point, the advantage is immediately taken,… sometimes, in spite of all that we can do, we go backwards instead of forwards.

Finally, on November 9, 1793, a full month after entering the Bay of Bengal, the *Kron Princessa Maria* pitched at anchor in the mouth of the Hooghly River, waiting for a pilot to come aboard and guide the ship up the river to Calcutta and Serampore beyond it. At the head of the Bay of Bengal, two mighty rivers, the Ganges and the Brahmaputra, fanned out to form a large delta. The Hooghly River was one of the many river branches that ran from the confluence of these two great rivers to the sea.

As the ship bobbed at anchor, many questions whirled around in William's mind. Where should they start their missionary work? Where would they all live? And what would the East India Company do when they found out that two Englishmen were preaching to Indians? William had read that there were only about fifteen hundred English people in the whole of India at that time, and most of them worked for the East India Company. How could they ever hope to go unnoticed for very long?

None of these questions, however, was as important as the gloomy question William did not even want to think about but knew he had to: How were they going to get past the East India Company officials on their way to Serampore? If they were discovered on their way up the river, they might not even be allowed to set foot in India, let alone preach there.

William peered over the side of the ship into the yellow river water. He reached into his pocket and pulled out a piece of paper. Somehow, he had to find a way to get around what was written on that paper.

Chapter 9

# On Indian Soil

William Carey sat at the desk in his cabin, turning the piece of paper in his hand over and over. Every few minutes he looked down and reread the words written on it. He hardly had to, though; he could recite them by heart:

> If any subject of His Majesty, not being lawfully licensed, should at any time repair to or be found in the East Indies, such persons were to be declared guilty of a high crime and misdemeanor, and be liable to fine and imprisonment....

As well, William had written on the page the text of an order issued by the rulers of British-controlled India. He reread those words, too:

> Every commander of a vessel arriving in India is to give to their pilot a faithful return of all passengers on board, and stating whether or not they have a license from the East India Company.
>
> Government of India, 1789

William wasn't sure what to do. He could not ask Captain Christmas to lie for him, nor could he risk being sent back to England. There had to be another way, but what was it?

As he mulled over the group's predicament, an idea popped into his mind. He quickly read the words of the government decree one more time. The answer had been there all along. It had just taken him a while to see it! Captain Christmas had to declare all passengers *on board.* But what if a passenger, or group of passengers, was to disembark before the ship took on a pilot? There was nothing in the decree that said that a passenger had to wait for a pilot to come aboard before disembarking. William smiled to himself. That was his answer. Quickly, he stood up and went to find Captain Christmas. Four hours later, the eight members of the missionary party were secretly hoisted over the side of the ship into a small native boat called a *pansi.*

The plan was for the group to meet up with Captain Christmas and the *Kron Princessa Maria* in Calcutta, where she would be docked for several days before heading farther upriver to Serampore.

The tide was with them as they began the journey up the Hooghly River. William was fascinated with everything he saw along the riverbanks. The women, many of them balancing baskets on their heads, wore brightly colored long dresses called *saris.* The gathered skirts swished gently as the women walked along. The men, on the other hand, had turbans wrapped around their heads, and they wore wide, floppy cotton pants called *pajamas.* William felt as if he'd walked into the pages of an adventure story.

Finally, when the tide turned and the pansi could no longer make headway against the strong current, the boatman told Dr. Thomas they would have to stop and begin their journey again in six hours, when the tide had turned in their favor.

William could scarcely believe it when he was at last standing by the side of the river with both feet planted firmly on Indian soil. The pansi had tied up beside a village marketplace, and William gazed at the amazing sight—like nothing he had ever seen in England. All around him, merchants sat or squatted next to large, flat baskets filled with vegetables and fruits, most of which he had never seen before. Other merchants were selling dried fish, and still others sold brass and silverware, bright-colored cotton fabrics, sandals, and some things he had no idea what possible use they were for. Around the merchants, people milled, bartering for a fair price for the goods they wanted to buy. The air in the marketplace was also filled with odors. Some were pungent and repulsive, but others were sweet and inviting. Some of the smells William recognized, but there were many he did not.

Within minutes, a crowd had gathered around them. Brown hands reached out to pinch little Jabez's cheeks and poke at the older boys. Dolly drew back, afraid of what might happen next. But there was nothing to be afraid of; it was just that most of the people had never before seen a white woman and her children alone without servants.

As the crowd gathered, William desperately wanted to preach to the assembled people, but he hadn't yet learned enough Bengali. Instead, he urged Dr. Thomas to preach. For the next three hours, that's exactly what Dr. Thomas did. As Dr. Thomas spoke, the residents of the village listened carefully. And when Dr. Thomas had said all he had to say, several people in the crowd brought a meal of curried vegetables and rice, proudly arranged on plantain leaf plates, for them all to eat. The villagers laughed among themselves as William, Dolly, and Kitty tried eating with their fingers for the first time. The visitors made quite a mess. The three oldest Carey boys, though, seemed to enjoy the new eating style, which brought a welcome change from the knives and forks they'd had to eat with at the captain's table aboard ship.

When they had all finished eating, William continued exploring the marketplace while Dr. Thomas answered the village residents' questions. Before William had run out of things to see, the boatmen yelled that the tide had turned and it was time to get under way again. Everyone climbed back in the pansi and continued on upriver toward Calcutta. As the missionaries cast off from the jetty, several people from the village yelled out that they would be welcome back anytime.

Back in the pansi, William and Dr. Thomas discussed their first missionary experience. William was thrilled at how long the Hindu people had stood and listened to the gospel message being preached, and he marveled at the intelligent questions they asked afterward. Over the next two days, the same scene repeated itself three more times in other villages before the pansi finally reached Calcutta.

The *Kron Princessa Maria* arrived soon after them, and the missionaries were able to collect their belongings and say farewell to Captain Christmas.

While the Carey family waited with their pile of belongings in an English-style tea shop near the Calcutta docks, Dr. Thomas went off in search of his wife and daughter. He was gone two hours before he returned with good news. His wife and daughter were both safe and well and living in a house they had rented near the center of town. In addition, Dr. Thomas brought back several servants to carry their belongings to the house where they could all stay.

After winding their way through streets lined with mud brick buildings and numerous bazaars and marketplaces, they came to a very English-looking street lined with trees on both sides. They stopped in front of house number 43. Dr. Thomas rang the doorbell. William could hear the sound echoing inside the house. Within moments, a servant swung the large wooden front door open. Behind the servant stood Mrs. Thomas and Eliza.

An hour later, after a change of clothes, the whole group was reunited in the parlor around a large mahogany table. They sipped tea and swapped stories of their trips from England and told of how they had entered India without a license. Mrs. Thomas explained that one of her friends was the wife of a high-ranking government officer, and since she and Eliza were traveling alone without Dr. Thomas, the officer had arranged a special entry permit for them both and had even loaned them the money to set up house.

As the reunited group talked, servants scurried in and out, bringing sandwiches and pots of tea. With each new pot of tea, one of the women servants would stretch out her arms to relieve Dolly of having to hold Jabez. Instead of handing him over, however, Dolly clung to her baby more tightly.

Despite his wife's fears, William was glad to be in India. He was also glad to see Dr. Thomas reunited with his family. But something bothered him about it all. He had come to India to share the gospel message with those who lived in the villages dotted across the landscape. He hoped the plush surroundings and servants were not the way Mrs. Thomas expected to live now that they had all arrived. Apart from anything else, they didn't have the money to support such a lifestyle!

By the next morning, Mrs. Thomas had directed the servants to unpack all the clothing trunks, and the boys were running up and down the stairs and in and out of the back veranda, happy to be on dry land again.

As the boys scurried about, William sat on the veranda examining a hibiscus. He marveled at the flower's intricate structure as he peered at it through his magnifying glass. As he studied the flower, he heard the front doorbell ring and then footsteps on the marble floor. Several minutes later, Dr. Thomas called his name. William took one last glance at the beautiful bloom under his magnifying glass and then headed inside. Waiting in the hallway was a tall Indian man wearing a white turban, green tunic, and white pants. The man bowed politely when he saw William.

"There you are," said Dr. Thomas with a beaming smile. "This is Ram Boshu, one of the three converts I told you so much about."

William's face lit up with a broad smile.

"It is an honor to meet you, sir," said Ram in perfect English. "As soon as I heard Dr. Thomas was back, I came to find my honored friend right away."

The three men went into the library to talk further. William pulled from his pocket a letter to Ram from the missionary society committee back in England. As Ram Boshu read the letter, his eyes filled with tears.

"I am not worthy to receive such kind Christian greetings," he confessed. "Since you left me, Dr. Thomas, I have been under much pressure from my family. They are always asking me to worship the family gods with them. After many weeks of serving Jesus Christ, I gave in and went with them to the temple. And now I am not worthy."

While dismayed that Ram had gone back to his

Hindu gods, William and Dr. Thomas felt that he sounded genuinely sorry over his actions. And since he spoke such good English, William asked him to become his *munshi,* or language teacher.

Now that he had someone to help him with the Bengali language, William was anxious to get on with the business of being a missionary. In his book, *Enquiry,* he had laid out principles for missionary work, and now it was time to put them into practice. First, he had to find a way to live as simply as possible among the Indian people, and second, he needed a way to support himself so that money could be freed up for the missionary society committee to send out more missionaries.

William knew it would take a while for this to happen, but the first step was to sell the goods they had brought to India. Dr. Thomas had previously assured him that the metal goods and lengths of woolen fabric could easily be sold to raise the one hundred fifty pounds it would cost them to live simply for a year. However, in the time that Dr. Thomas had been away from India, there had been a glut on the market of the very items William had brought, and so the sale of the goods raised nowhere near the amount of money expected.

It took only two weeks for the missionary group to realize that their money was going too quickly. They would have to rethink their plans. After much discussion, and over the protest of all three women, it was decided that they would move to the Portuguese settlement of Bandel, thirty miles farther on up the Hooghly River from Calcutta, where living costs would be much lower.

Since it was much faster to travel by pansi up the river than to go overland to Bandel, the group, joined by Eliza, Mrs. Thomas, and Ram Boshu, found themselves once again on the move. It took three days to cover the distance, but the farther upstream they got, away from the influence of the tide, the faster they were able to go.

Once in Bandel, William and Dr. Thomas, accompanied by Ram Boshu, went in search of a place to live. They found a small but adequate house, which they rented. The six members of the Carey family and Kitty shared one room, the three Thomases shared the second room, and Ram slept in a tiny room at the back of the house that had once been a large cupboard.

As soon as they were settled in, William purchased a map of the area and began planning the trips he and Dr. Thomas would take. The two men bought a small boat, and within a few days, they were off sharing the gospel message in the villages that dotted the banks of the Hooghly River. Wherever they went, crowds, sometimes as large as two or three hundred people, came to hear them. At first, Dr. Thomas did the preaching, but within a week, William could speak the Bengali language well enough to preach by himself. Now he was beginning to feel like a real missionary.

William loved the life of a missionary in Bandel, but it was not to last. The problem was Dr. Thomas.

Because Dr. Thomas had lived in India before, William had unwisely left him in charge of the money. But by mid-December, just four weeks after arriving in Bandel, the situation was grim. With eleven mouths to feed, their money was almost completely gone. Something had to be done.

They had set aside a small sum of money to establish a permanent mission station, but no matter how desperate things might get, William and Dr. Thomas had pledged not to touch this money until it was needed for that purpose.

As William pondered what to do, he received a letter from Captain Christmas. The captain had heard of a vacancy for a head gardener at the East India Botanical Gardens in Calcutta. Remembering how much William knew about botany, he had recommended him for the job. The recommendation had been approved, and William Carey could have the job if he wanted it. Better still, the job came with a house! The same day, Dr. Thomas received word that some of his creditors were still after him. It was decided that the whole group would pack up and move back to Calcutta, where William would work as a botanist and Dr. Thomas would open a medical office and earn some money to pay back his creditors. Each family would live separately, and once they were established, they would find ways to continue their missionary work.

It was a great plan. It just didn't work. When William went to see about the job at the botanical gardens, he was told there had been a misunderstanding and the position had already been given to someone else. Now the Carey family had no place to live and very little money. William wasn't sure what to do. Thankfully, Ram Boshu did. He had a banker friend who agreed to let the Careys stay in a small garden house on the back of his property in Manicktulla. Manicktulla was in a large swampy area northeast of the city and came complete with malaria-carrying mosquitoes and bands of robbers who roamed the muddy streets. The Careys, though, were never bothered by the robbers, probably because they looked like they had nothing worth stealing.

Soon after arriving in Manicktulla, Dolly, Felix, and William Jr. all became sick with dysentery. As the days dragged on, Dolly and Kitty began to complain about everything. The weather was too hot. They were bored and lonely for English company. The local people frightened them. The language was too hard to learn. The children were restless. Their stomachs couldn't get used to the steady diet of vegetables and rice, and they wondered why Indians ate chapatis instead of good bread. They also blamed Dr. Thomas for getting them into the mess they were in.

The complaining and questioning went on day and night. In the end, William wrote in his diary: "My wife, and sister too, who do not see the importance of the mission as I do, are continually exclaiming against me.... If my family were but hearty in the work, I should find a great burden removed."

No matter how poor they were or how desperate their situation, William was grateful that Dr. Thomas had put away a little money for missionary work. He told himself he wouldn't use the money to buy food for the family but would instead spend it to print Bibles or pay for the setting up of a permanent mission station. This still left William with the problem of how to earn the money needed to feed and keep his family in the meantime. He had to come up with a solution, and fast. It was early January, just two months since they had arrived in India, and already the family was down to its last bag of rice.

Two weeks went by. William stretched the rice as far as it would go, but it was all but gone. Just when he began to despair that they might all starve, Ram Boshu arrived with some good news. His uncle had offered William and his family the use of some land, rent free for three years. The land was located in Dechatta, forty miles east of Calcutta. There William could plant a garden and grow vegetables so that the family could become self-sufficient. But to get the family there and purchase the needed seed and supplies would cost money. However, since the place would serve as a permanent base for his missionary work, William decided to use the money Dr. Thomas had set aside for missionary work. With it he would buy the necessary provisions and pay for the transport of his family to Dechatta. First thing in the morning, he would go to Calcutta to visit Dr. Thomas and collect the money.

Chapter 10

# Into the Sunderbans

William Carey shook his friend's hand and walked out through the huge wrought iron gates. Once he was out of sight of the mansion, he stopped and leaned against a mud brick wall. He put his hands over his face and forced himself to think about what he had just seen and heard.

William had just visited Dr. Thomas's new office in one of the English sections of Calcutta. Nothing had prepared him for what happened during the visit. Dr. Thomas was living in luxury! He had rented a large home with beautiful new inlaid wood furniture and twelve servants. He was even talking about buying his own coach. That had been surprise enough, but when William asked for the missionary money so that he and his family could move out to the parcel of land they had been promised, Dr. Thomas cheerfully told him the whole amount had been spent. It got worse. Not only was all the money gone, but also Dr. Thomas had borrowed money in the name of the mission and had already spent that, too!

William was speechless. How could a man so brilliant be so foolish? And not only that, but Dr. Thomas was no longer sure he wanted to continue being a missionary, since the whole venture did not suit his wife. She—and, William suspected, Dr. Thomas as well—liked being a respected member of the English community. Being a missionary and living in a shack somewhere, swatting mosquitoes, and telling Indian people about the gospel message was not the way to earn that respect.

Right there on the street, thinking about his ill-fated visit, William decided not to tell Dolly or Kitty what had happened. It would only give them ammunition to fire back at him. However, he would have to send a letter to the missionary society committee and explain how they had completely run out of money in just ten weeks.

That night, after the others had gone to bed, William sat silently in the small garden house agonizing over what to tell his friends back in England. He wanted to say that he still appreciated many things about Dr. Thomas but now understood that Dr. Thomas was not the right man to send to start a mission. Dr. Thomas was filled with enthusiasm but little common sense. Slowly in his mind,

William formed the words he wanted to say, and then he wrote them down:

> Mr. Thomas is a very good man, but only fit to live at sea, where his daily business is before him and daily provision made for him. I fear his present undertaking will be hurtful rather than useful.... I love him, and we live in greatest harmony; but I confess that Ram Boshu is much more a man after my heart.

That night, William went to bed with a heavy heart. He had no friends, no money, and little food. As he drifted off to sleep, he decided the best thing to do was to set his pride aside and visit the army chaplain at Fort William, five miles away. Perhaps a fellow minister would know how to help. Of course, by going there he also ran the risk of arrest for being in India without a license.

Early the next morning, William set off to visit the chaplain. It was a hot, tiring walk to Fort William, so William set a slow pace. Along the way, he planned what he would say to the Reverend Brown, the army chaplain. He would explain to him how he intended to be self-sufficient and make just about everything his family needed and that he had been offered some land rent-free where he could do all this. Then he would ask the chaplain whether he knew of a way to get his family to Dechatta, where the land was located.

He arrived at Fort William around lunchtime, exhausted from the walk and from a lack of food.

The Reverend Brown met him at the door, and William explained his situation. He made the mistake, however, of mentioning Dr. Thomas's name. The Reverend Brown said some unkind words about the man and slammed the door in William's face.

As he trudged home with not so much as a glass of cold water in his stomach, William considered what had happened. Evidently, the Reverend Brown had already had a run-in with Dr. Thomas and was not about to help anyone associated with him. William understood the chaplain's feelings and determined to hold no grudge against him. That night his journal entry read:

> I am much dejected.... I am in a strange land, alone, no Christian friends, a large family, and nothing to supply their wants. I blame Mr. Thomas for leading me into such expense at first, and I blame myself for being led.... I am dejected, not for my own sake, but for my family's and his, for whom I tremble.

Ram Boshu brought a ray of hope into the gloomy situation the next morning when he arrived with a bag of rice for the family. The last of their rice had run out the day before, and the Carey boys' faces lit up as Ram laid the sack down. William was grateful for the rice, but he was preoccupied with what to do next. Finally, he decided the only option left was to find someone who would lend him money. Coming to such a decision, though, made it one of the worst days in his life. Even in England, when he had almost nothing, William had never borrowed money. Now he was left with no alternative, and the realization gnawed at his empty stomach more than the hunger pangs he'd been enduring to stretch the rice supply as far as possible.

That afternoon, he walked into Calcutta in search of someone to lend him money, but he found no one. Nor did he the next day. Not a single banker in the whole city would lend him a rupee. More dejected than ever, William walked home, ate a bowl of rice, and went to bed.

The next day, January 31, 1794, there was a knock on the rickety door of the garden house. When William answered it, there stood Dr. Thomas, who explained that after thinking about things for a few days, he felt guilty about what had happened. He had borrowed one hundred fifty rupees in his own name for William's family, enough money to buy the needed supplies and get the family to Dechatta.

William lost no time packing up the family and preparing to move. The sooner he got to Dechatta, the sooner he could start his garden and feed his family. The following day, Saturday, he and Ram Boshu went to the main bazaar in the city to buy seed and a shovel, plus enough food for the trip. On Sunday, they both went back to the bazaar, this time to preach to the people. On Monday, they bought a small boat, and on Tuesday morning, the Carey family, accompanied by Ram Boshu, climbed into the boat and set off for their new home.

Dolly and Kitty were not at all pleased with the situation. They feared what lay ahead and complained constantly about "being forced to go out into the wilderness!" And they had a right to be worried. Going to the Sunderbans, as the area around Dechatta was called, was a desperate move. The Sunderbans was made up of a network of tidal rivers and streams that crisscrossed the huge delta formed by the Ganges and Brahmaputra rivers before they emptied into the Bay of Bengal. It was a wild and dangerous place to live.

William tried to keep the group's spirits up as he and Ram Boshu slowly poled the boat along the forty miles of jungle waterways that lay between Calcutta and Dechatta. The scenery along the way was not like anything William had seen before. The rice fields surrounded by thickets of bamboo and tall waving palm trees fascinated him. The children were interested, too, at least for the first day. By the third day, though, everyone was hot and cranky.

At night, they pulled the boat over to the side of the river and slept. No one got much sleep, however, because of the many noises and shadows moving among the trees. Bengal tigers prowled the riverbanks, as did leopards, rhinoceroses, and buffaloes. Monkeys screeched in the treetops, and pythons and cobras slithered quietly through the long grass.

By day, as William and Ram Boshu poled along, they would catch glimpses of large crocodiles sunning themselves lazily on the muddy riverbank. For every crocodile they spotted, they knew there were a dozen more lurking in the muddy water. Mosquitoes, tiny as they were, were as much a problem as the larger animals. Within a day of leaving, the boys all had open sores from scratching at the insect bites.

On the third morning, Ram Boshu guided the boat into the Jubona River, and soon afterward, they arrived at the village of Dechatta, where Ram went to find his uncle. Soon they were all back in the boat for the half-hour trip farther up the river to the land they had been promised. Finally, Ram pointed out the site to them. It was nothing more than a patch of jungle, but William was determined to make a farm out of it. It would take time, however, and time was something they didn't have. They had spent all their money on supplies and had just eaten the last of their food on the journey. Still, William was undeterred. He would just have to work harder and faster at clearing the jungle and planting a garden.

A little farther up the river on the opposite bank stood a sturdy-looking brick bungalow. William decided to find out who lived there before he and his family disembarked at their new home. They poled the boat up to the tiny jetty in front of the house and tied it up, and they all climbed out. The boys were glad to be able to run around, though Dolly fussed after them if they went more than a few feet away from her. As the whole bedraggled band walked up the path to the house, the door swung open, and an Englishman came striding out to meet them. He shook William's hand heartily and introduced himself as Charles Short. Of course, he was surprised to see an English family so far out in the Sunderbans and immediately invited them all in for lunch.

Over the meal, served on the veranda, William and Mr. Short swapped stories of why they were in India. Mr. Short told the group he had come out from London to take charge of the East India Company's salt factory at Dechatta. William, in turn, told him about being a missionary. As he did so, Mr. Short laughed out loud. "How ever do you expect to do missionary work in a land with such strong religious rules?" he asked William. Then he added, "And why bother? Isn't it better to leave everyone with their own religion?"

William thought of the idols and temples he had seen since arriving in India and of the human sacrifice he'd heard about and shook his head. "God has called me to these heathen people, and I will gladly give my life trying to reach them with the gospel message."

Mr. Short leaned back in his chair thoughtfully. "I can't say I agree with you one bit. I'm not a God-fearing man myself, but you are in need of a place to stay, and I have a large house, as you can see. Stay with me as long as you need, and I will have the cook make meals for us all." His eyes twinkled as he spoke, and then he added, "It's been a long time since I've had some lively conversation, and I think a Baptist parson should provide that."

William thanked Mr. Short for his kind offer, and the group brought their belongings up to the house from the boat. It was a great relief for William to know that his wife and sons would have a roof over their heads and food every day. William said a silent prayer of thanks as he carried the last of their belongings inside. He also promised himself that the family would not overstay their welcome. The following day, at first light, he and Ram Boshu would begin clearing the jungle on their property.

Later that evening, after a wonderful meal of lamb stew and bread and while Dolly and Kitty put the boys to bed and Mr. Short did some paperwork, William and Ram Boshu sat on the veranda talking.

"I have been talking to the gardener," Ram said nervously. "He says the locals have all left the area. The only ones left are those who work for Mr. Short in the salt factory."

"Did he say why they left?" asked William in a low voice.

Ram nodded, his voice fell to a whisper. "Tigers. The area is infested with tigers."

William gulped and looked over his shoulder toward the surrounding jungle.

Ram went on. "In the last three months, twenty men in the area have been killed by them. Now people are too afraid to work outdoors."

"It's good to know what we are up against," replied William, trying to sound undeterred, and then added, "All the more reason to pray as we work!"

It took several weeks for William and Ram Boshu to clear enough land to build a hut and plant a garden. Ram arranged for the timber they cut down to be sold at a nearby market to raise money for the family to buy much-needed supplies. As they worked, Ram went over Bengali words and phrases with William. At the same time, they both kept a constant eye out for the telltale stripes of a tiger moving amongst the surrounding jungle. William's rifle was always at his side. Although he didn't see any tigers, on several occasions William shot a wild pig or a deer for everyone at the house to eat.

Surprisingly, as William labored out under the hot Indian sun, he never once itched. The painful rash he used to get when he was out in the sun in England never recurred in India.

After three weeks, the new hut was nearly ready to move into, though William had a tough time getting the women to consider moving into it. After all, they would be trading a brick, English-style home, with plenty of food and servants to cook it, for a bamboo hut with grass-mat flooring and a thatched roof! Indeed, Dolly did not like to leave Mr. Short's house at any time. She spent hours sitting in a corner singing softly to herself. Often she ignored the children for long periods of time and didn't seem to hear William when he tried to coax her out to eat a meal with the others.

William had to face the fact that Dolly's mental condition was getting worse. He tried to do what he could for her, but in 1794, there was not much that could be done. Kitty watched over the children and often took them to visit Mr. Short at the salt factory. She always had a servant accompany them because she was terrified of meeting a wild animal on the short boat trip.

William, on the other hand, had little time for visiting. He had to get a garden planted as quickly as possible so that it could start producing food for the family. At the same time, he and Ram Boshu took every opportunity they could to go downstream in their boat to nearby villages and share the gospel message.

After one such visit, William came home shaken by what he had seen. He and Ram had tied up their boat at a village where a large, cheering crowd had gathered. After inching his way to the front, William was horrified by what he saw. There, about six feet off the ground was a man being swung around in circles. The man was hanging from a rope suspended from a long bamboo pole. The men of the village took turns running around underneath him and spinning him or holding up the ends of the pole. All of this would have done nothing more than make the swinging man a little dizzy, except for one thing. The man was attached to the rope by two hooks that were jabbed through his bare back. He was hanging by his flesh. William had to look away. He had read about this practice, but to see a man actually hurting himself as an act of worship to Siva, a Hindu god, made him sick to his stomach.

The man swung on the hooks from the rope for over fifteen minutes before he was finally lowered to the ground bleeding and grimacing in pain. William longed to be able to give the villagers the gospel message and tell them about how God loved them.

About this time, William came to the conclusion that preaching to the Indian people alone would not be enough. The Hindu religion in particular possessed many ancient books of sacred writing that Hindus revered and followed. If Christian missionaries were to be successful in the country, William knew that the Bible needed to be translated as quickly as possible into the various Indian languages. He decided it was time to once again get to work on the Bengali translation of the Book of Genesis that he and Dr. Thomas had begun on the journey from England.

As he was finishing work on the Carey family's new bamboo hut, William heard some good news. Word had spread around the district that there was now a white man with a gun building a house near Dechatta. This gave the local people who had fled the area renewed confidence, and many of them began to return. Soon William was surrounded by Indian people, many of whom were interested in hearing the gospel message. After all the setbacks, William was greatly encouraged, especially when a party of five Brahmins (upper-caste Hindus) came and thanked him for settling among them. Surely, Dechatta was the open door to missionary work William had been searching for!

## Chapter 11

# Mudnabatti

Unbeknownst to William, at the same time he had been desperately seeking money and support for his family in Calcutta before finally moving to Dechatta, an event had occurred in a dangerous channel of the Hooghly River near Malda, one hundred twenty miles to the north. The event, tragic as it was, would change the course of William's life in India.

The event was a boating accident in which two English people, Robert Udney and his wife, were drowned. The couple had just moved to Dinadjpur Province to work with Robert's brother, George. George Udney lived in Malda, where he was commercial resident for the East India Company. This meant that he was the most powerful English person in the area. George Udney was responsible for improving agriculture and industry in the province. He was able to make loans and help start new farming and industrial projects.

George Udney was also a good Christian who knew Dr. Thomas from his previous visit to India. As was the case with many of Dr. Thomas's friends, George Udney had loaned him money, which Dr. Thomas had never repaid. This had caused a rift in their friendship. However, when Dr. Thomas read of the drownings in the newspaper, he immediately wrote to his "friend" to say how sorry he was to hear of his brother's death.

Being a forgiving man, when he received the letter from Dr. Thomas, George Udney wrote back and invited him to visit Malda. Dr. Thomas did so, and the two men became friends again. During his visit, Dr. Thomas told how he was not doing well in Calcutta. Yes, he was making good money as a doctor, but the problem was that he and his wife were still spending more than they made. He longed for a simpler life. George Udney had just the answer to his problem. He explained that his dead brother had been given the job of overseer at one of two new indigo-dye factories being built in the province. Now that his brother was dead, George had to find someone else to run the factory and wondered whether Dr. Thomas might be interested in the position. A large house and generous salary came with the job, plus Dr. Thomas would get a small share of any profit the factory made.

Dr. Thomas immediately accepted the position and then asked whether George Udney had anyone in mind to run the second factory. George Udney did not, but Dr. Thomas knew just the man for the job.

"Papa, papa, there is a letter for you," yelled nine-year-old Felix as he ran up the path to Mr. Short's house waving an envelope.

William was on the veranda working on the translation of the Book of Genesis that he and Dr. Thomas had begun. He smiled broadly as his son ran up with the envelope. At last, after six months in India, a letter! He was not sure whom he would most like it to be from, his friends on the missionary society committee or his father. It was from neither.

As he took the envelope from Felix and turned it over, William immediately recognized the handwriting—the same handwriting he'd just been reading, that of Dr. Thomas. William tore open the letter and began to read. The more he read, the more excited he became. George Udney, commercial resident for Dinadjpur Province, had offered him a job overseeing an indigo dye factory. And the job came with a house and two hundred fifty pounds a year as salary! The salary alone was five times as much as William had ever earned before. William did some fast math in his head and discovered that his whole family could easily live on a quarter of the amount, leaving over one hundred eighty pounds per year to put toward translating and printing the entire Bible in Bengali. More than that, Dr. Thomas pointed out that George Udney was a godly man who understood that William would want time off to preach to the local people and continue his translation work. As well, if he accepted the job, George Udney would get him a five-year permit to work in India. William would no longer have to worry about being caught and sent to jail in England. It all sounded almost too good to be true.

William thought about all the wonderful opportunities the job would give him. The letter had stated that the factory would employ ninety workers, and William felt sure that he would have the chance to share the gospel message with each worker. It was a thrilling prospect. Of course, he would miss Dechatta, which was already beginning to feel like home. But somehow the job offer seemed to William to be God's direction for him and his family. "Just think," he told Dolly, "we won't have to worry about money for food anymore!" And then he wrote in his journal: "This appears to be a remarkable opening in divine providence, for our comfortable support."

May 23, 1794, was moving day, but not into the bamboo hut that William had labored to build. Instead, William was headed with his family up the Hooghly River to Malda to meet George Udney and begin work in the indigo dye factory.

Despite the wonderful job that awaited her husband, Dolly Carey was not eager to leave Mr. Short's house, for good reasons. First, the journey itself was a dangerous one. It involved poling their boat two hundred miles in one-hundred-ten-degree heat in the height of mosquito season. Second, her sister Kitty would not be traveling with them. Kitty and Mr. Short had fallen in love and planned to marry the following year. This meant that Dolly would be in charge of the boys for three or four weeks on a boat no bigger than a full-sized bed.

And what if the job didn't work out? Dolly asked William this question many times. After all, they had moved back to Calcutta to the job at the botanical gardens only to find it was already taken. What if there were a similar mix-up with this job? If that happened, they would be in a much worse situation than if they had stayed in Dechatta.

William was determined that it was the right thing to do. So, early in the morning, they said farewell to Kitty and Mr. Short and climbed aboard their little boat. It was difficult for the boys to say good-bye. They clung to their Aunt Kitty, who, in many ways, had been more of a mother to them than Dolly had been. But finally, after many tears, they got under way.

The trip to Malda took twenty-two long, hot days. Dolly and Felix were still suffering from the effects of dysentery and spent most of the time lying in the center of the boat under the full shade of the straw canopy that stretched most of the length of the craft. Even in the shade, the temperature hovered around one hundred degrees. It was so hot that the other children, who were not sick, hardly had the energy to sit up. In the evenings, they would tie the boat up beside a village. William and Ram Boshu would spend an hour or so preaching in the village while Dolly and the children did their best to set up camp for the night. The food for the journey consisted mostly of curried vegetables and rice, which they purchased from the many vendors along the well-traveled waterway.

As they traveled, William heard many people speaking in Hindustani, the language of the lower castes, and he immediately began to take notes on how to translate the Bible into it.

Progress on the journey was slow and reminded William of the month when the *Kron Princessa Maria* had tacked her way up the Bay of Bengal. This time, though, the trip was slow not because of the wind conditions but because of the shape of the rivers they were traveling. The entire Bengal region was a giant alluvial plain, across which the rivers sluggishly meandered, almost doubling back on themselves in places. Sometimes it took William and Ram Boshu two whole days to make four miles in a straight line!

On June 7, the boat reached the town of Bassetpore, where they purchased some square sails and rigged their boat for sailing. This made the rest of the trip much faster, but it also meant that they couldn't "feel" their way along the bottom as they had been able to when poling the boat. As a result, they were constantly running aground on the many shallow sandbars in the nine-mile-wide river.

On June 15, William Carey wrote in his journal: "I feel now as if released from a prison." The prison was the boat. They had made it safely to Malda, where they were greeted by George Udney and his mother, who lived with him. The two welcomed the group into their house for a large meal, and then one of their servants supervised the children while Dolly rested and William went over the job contract with George Udney.

Much to his relief, William found that for once Dr. Thomas had not exaggerated. George Udney was a wonderful Christian who cared deeply about the Indian men who worked for him. He told William that as long as everything ran smoothly at the factory, he was free to take as much time as he liked to do his Bible translation work.

That evening, after a delicious supper of venison, William wrote to the missionary society committee. With great joy he told them about the new job. He asked the committee not to send him any more money, although he hadn't yet received any they might have already sent. Instead, he urged them to send out another missionary with the money they had set aside to support him and his family. Finally, everything was working out the way he had imagined it would.

The Careys stayed with George Udney and his mother for two weeks. It took that much time to coax Dolly back into the boat and for George Udney to answer all William's questions about the indigo factory and the dye-making process. There was so much to learn, and William did not want to make any mistakes. George Udney patiently explained that it would soon be monsoon season and that was when indigo dye making began. For three months, starting the end of July, *Indigofera Tinctoria* (indigo) plants that had been planted in March were cut down at the stalk, and the whole plants were bundled up and brought to the factory on bullock carts. There, the indigo plants were soaked in huge vats of water.

While in the water, the plants were beaten to release the blue dye. To do this, the Indian workers stripped naked and waded into the vats, beating the water with huge bamboo paddles. At just the right moment, the water had to be drained from the vats and the leaves strained out, leaving behind the liquid indigo that had settled at the bottom of the vat. The mixture was then left to ferment before the remaining liquid was evaporated off, leaving behind solid cakes of indigo dye. The cakes were then cut into chunks and transported to Calcutta to be sold locally or shipped to Europe. Indigo, William learned, was in high demand because it dyed fabrics such a bright shade of blue. In fact, the blue coats worn by American soldiers during the American Revolution had been made from fabric dyed with indigo.

During his stay in Malda, William was asked to preach at the small church service held each Sunday in George Udney's home. Just the thought of a church service reminded William of how lonely he had really been for Christian fellowship. On Sunday, sixteen English people, including Dr. Thomas, arrived for the service.

Afterward, William and Dr. Thomas talked privately. William forgave Dr. Thomas for the problems he had caused with the money and agreed that now everything was starting to work out well. The two men also talked about translating the Bible into Bengali. William was determined to keep working on the project during the nine months when there was no indigo dye production.

Finally, after two weeks, it was time for the Carey family and Ram Boshu to climb back into their boat and head thirty-two miles up the River Tangan to Mudnabatti, where the factory William would be overseeing was located. The current was strong, and the journey took three days. The factory Dr. Thomas was overseeing was located at Moypaldiggy, another seventeen miles on up the river past Mudnabatti.

When the Careys finally arrived, they found things much as George Udney had described them. A large two-story brick house with large venetian windows was set back just a little from the riverbank. Several servants dressed in white came scurrying out as soon as the boat tied up at the jetty. Inside, the house was furnished with everything an English family could want. For the first time since leaving England a year before, William Carey breathed a sigh of relief. His family was safe, they had a strong home and plenty to eat, and most important, he had enough money left over to continue his translation and missionary work. Things were beginning to look up.

The three older Carey boys loved their new home. From their upstairs bedroom they could see bright green rice fields stretching for miles in every direction. Spread out among the rice fields were small villages in the shade of huge mango and banyan trees. Unlike the jungle at Dechatta, there weren't many wild animals prowling near the house, except snakes. They soon learned not to walk too close to thickets of prickly pear bushes. Deadly cobras lived among them, and a cobra's bite meant certain death, often in less than an hour.

William had been in the new home a month when the monsoon rains began signaling it was time to harvest the indigo plants. He pulled out all the notes he had taken during his conversations with George Udney and prepared to set to work making dye.

The night before the factory was to open, William looked outside his dining room window and saw a group of men he had just hired coming toward the house. They were carrying a struggling baby goat between them. William hurried outside to see what they wanted.

"It is time for the factory to open," began one of the men in Bengali.

William nodded with a puzzled look on his face, wondering where such a statement was leading.

"Then you must come with us, Sahib, " the man continued on. "It is time for you to make the sacrifice to Kali. See, we have brought the offering with us." He pointed in the direction of the young goat.

Now William understood what they wanted. He had seen statues of Kali, a huge, ugly Hindu goddess with four arms, a tongue that stuck out, and a belt draped around her waist with human skulls hanging from it. Kali was the goddess of destruction. William took a deep breath and said, "Kali is your goddess of destruction. You make sacrifices you cannot afford to her because you are scared she will destroy your crops, kill your families, and blow your homes away. I am not scared of these things, because I serve a God who loves me. I will not make sacrifices to a god who destroys things. The Living God gives life; He does not ask for us to take it."

The Indians nodded quietly as William explained to them more about God and the Bible. William learned the next morning, however, that they sacrificed the goat anyway. When William came down with a bad case of malaria a month later, many of the Indian workers decided that it was Kali paying him back for his lack of respect.

Dolly and Felix continued their slow recovery from dysentery. The sickness had left them both weak and thin. Then in September, just as the last batch of indigo had been crated and put on boats for Calcutta, five-year-old Peter came down with dysentery. His small body was not able to resist the disease, and he died within hours.

William and Dolly were heartbroken, and since they were both ill themselves, they sent Ram Boshu out to find someone to make a coffin for their son. There were several carpenters among the men who worked at the factory, and William felt sure that one of them would be willing to help out, especially since he paid them well. But every one of them refused to help. They were all Hindus and would have nothing to do with a dead white person's body. This was because of caste, the strict system of rules that forbade different groups of Hindus from doing certain tasks. If they did them, they would be breaking caste and would be thrown out of their families and villages. Handling the dead body of a Christian was against the rules for all Hindu castes. The experience demonstrated for William the strong grip the caste system had over every Hindu. When he recovered, William wrote in his journal: "Perhaps the caste system is one of the strongest chains with which the devil ever bound the children of men. This is my comfort, that God can break it."

In the meantime, William Carey lay in bed too ill to do anything but pray that someone would have compassion on a family who had just lost one of its members. Because of the heat, it was necessary for Peter's body to be buried the same day. But who was going to do it? Finally, Ram Boshu found four Moslem men who agreed to make a coffin for Peter and dig a grave in which to bury him.

Peter had been a bright little child, and like his father, he loved to learn new things. He could also speak Bengali like a native. While William grieved for him, his death had a much more devastating effect on Dolly. At other times when she had experienced great tragedy, like the death of her two daughters, she had taken a long time to recover emotionally. But after Peter's death, she did not recover. Perhaps it was the strain of not having Kitty to help her, or the trauma of knowing people would not help with the funeral, or her own long bout with dysentery. For whatever reason, Dolly sank deeper into sadness and depression.

William, too, was also beginning to feel the effects of depression, but for a different reason. He had been in India for fourteen months now and still had not received one letter from England. He was feeling cut off and lonely.

## Chapter 12

# Spies!

Surely you have not forgotten us?" William Carey wrote in his careful handwriting. He hoped those on the missionary society committee were still "holding the ropes" for him back in England as they had promised. But it was hard to believe that fourteen months after arriving in India he still hadn't received a single letter from any of them, or from anyone else in England for that matter!

What William didn't know was that the war between England and France had grown worse. As a result, the French privateers had become bolder. They were no longer content just to plunder off the English coast. Now they lay in wait for British ships all along the trade route to India. By the middle of 1794, two out of every three ships sailing from

Calcutta were being boarded and looted by French pirates. Not only had William not received any letters from the committee, but the committee had not received any of the letters he had written to them.

During the remaining nine months of the year when indigo dye was not being produced, William visited the two hundred small villages that surrounded Mudnabatti. He inspected the fields where the indigo plants were grown and stayed on to talk with the people about their Hindu gods.

Dr. Thomas was just as busy in Moypaldiggy running a free medical clinic. It was the only clinic for miles, and Dr. Thomas's house was surrounded day and night by sick people begging for help.

Both William and Dr. Thomas used some of their money to start a boarding school, which was attended by twelve young men. Among the subjects taught were geography, science, and Bible study. Ram Boshu was the principal, and the two missionaries paid for all the boys' needs. The three men hoped to train up Christian leaders for the Bengal district.

William had made great strides in translating the Bible into Bengali. He had also set himself the task of learning Sanskrit. While the Sanskrit language was very difficult to learn, William had begun to see its importance. Sanskrit was an ancient language that had originated in India about 1000 B.C. Many European languages, such as Latin, English, Greek, and German, had words with Sanskrit roots. The Bengali language also had many Sanskrit words in it, which was one reason William began learning it.

If he could understand Sanskrit, it would be easier for him to unlock the meaning of Bengali words. William had another reason for wanting to learn the language. Almost all of the classical Indian writing was in Sanskrit, and William realized that if he wanted to reach the educated people of India with the Bible, he would have to translate it into the same language as their classical religious writings. And so he busied himself learning the language.

William was grateful that he worked for the East India Company because by 1796, company officials had become even more determined to round up missionaries and other unwanted English people and return them to England. William's job meant that he could go about his missionary work without fear of being sent home.

Yet, for all his work, William felt frustrated because he had not won a single Indian convert to Christianity. He had no difficulty attracting a crowd of two or three hundred people who would sit politely and listen to him for hours. But there were no converts. William held a short service each morning with his factory workers, who all nodded enthusiastically when he told them about how God could save them from their sins. But still no converts. Even Ram Boshu, who had sacrificed so much to help William with his Bible translation and missionary work, was unwilling to shut the door completely on the Hindu gods and be baptized.

At least things were going a little better at home, though. After more than a year and half of deep depression, Dolly's condition improved a little, and she became pregnant again. In 1796, when William was thirty-five years old, Dolly gave birth to their seventh baby, another boy, whom they named Jonathan. Much to everyone's relief, Jonathan was a chubby, healthy child right from the start. His arrival made both William and Dolly very happy.

In all his letters back to England, William continually mentioned the need to send more missionaries to India. There was enough work in the Bengal region alone to keep a thousand missionaries busy. In his letters, William also suggested to the committee that future missionaries be sent out as assistant indigo-dye factory overseers. That way they would be granted an entry permit and be allowed to come and work with him.

One day in late 1796, as William was bent over his desk studying Sanskrit, he heard a knock at the door. William opened the door to find his Indian neighbor and a young white man standing there.

"Here is a man from England," said the neighbor in Bengali. "I found him in Malda asking where your house was, so I brought him here to you."

William sprang forward, eager to meet another Englishman. "Welcome to my house," he said, as he reached for the man's hand and shook it. "It's wonderful to see a fellow countryman. Sit down. Tell me who you are and why you're here."

"My name is John Fountain," began the tall stranger. "I'm the missionary society's new recruit!"

The neighbor excused himself, and for the next few hours, the two Englishmen peppered each other with questions. William learned that John Fountain was from Rutland, in the next county to Northamptonshire, and knew many of William's friends. John Fountain was also a man after William's own heart. He had left his fiancé behind, and to save money for the committee, he had served as a servant on the voyage to India. And according to his entry permit, he had come to India to be an assistant overseer of the indigo dye factory in Mudnabatti.

John Fountain turned out to be a good factory overseer, too. Having him take over a number of the factory responsibilities meant that William could put in longer hours on his translation work.

By March 1797, William's initial translation of the Bible into Bengali was complete and ready to print. The question was how and where to print it. The original plan had been to send the finished manuscript back to England for printing, but with the number of French pirates prowling for English ships, this no longer seemed like a good idea. It took a year of mulling before William became convinced that the new translation of the Bible should be printed in India. To aid this process, George Udney purchased a secondhand printing press in Calcutta for William.

"The printing press will be here in a month," William excitedly told John Fountain. "It is being sent up the river on a barge, but there's much to do to prepare for its arrival. I'm thinking of setting it up in the dining room, right under the window for natural light."

As the news of what William was up to spread through the district, a friend offered to lend him enough money to buy the type and paper needed to produce one thousand copies of the Bible. (Because of the size of the translation, each Bible would actually consist of four separate books.) William planned to sell half the Bibles produced to pay back the loan, and then he would give away the rest.

William waited anxiously for the press to arrive. When it finally did, he was so excited that the Indian servants decided that the machine must have some magic, and they called it "Sahib's idol." William longed for them to understand that, far from being an idol, the press was going to produce books that would tell people how to free themselves from idols.

After the press was set up in his dining room, William decided to make the trip to Calcutta himself to buy the lead type he needed for printing. Along the way, he witnessed an event he'd only heard about up till then.

One evening, after he and a helper had moored their boat at a village for the night, William took a short walk along the riverbank. He saw a large crowd of excited people gathering. Wondering what could attract such a crowd, William wormed his way to the front, where he saw a large pile of wood. On top of the pile was the body of a dead man. Beside it was a woman dressed in white. The woman danced as if in a trance and threw little packages of food into the crowd from a basket she was carrying. William watched as people scrambled to pick them up.

With chilling clarity, William suddenly realized what he was about to witness: *sati,* the Hindu practice whereby a wife was burned on the funeral pyre with her dead husband. It was a common practice, because Hindus believed that if a wife died beside her husband, it would carry him and his entire family fourteen steps closer to heaven.

Right there, William began to preach. He pleaded with the crowd not to allow the woman to kill herself. He begged the woman to reconsider, telling her he would look after her if she would walk away. But she would not, and within minutes she lay quietly down on top of the body of her dead husband and placed her arm around his neck. Thick bamboo poles were clamped over them both so that there was no way the woman could move or escape. A hot butter called *ghee* was poured over them both, and then with a great *whoosh,* the fire was started. "Hurree-bol, hurree-bol," the crowd began shouting. The words were a Hindu shout for joy.

William felt sick to his stomach, and he turned to walk back to the boat. Whatever happened, he promised himself that night, he would find some way to stop the dreadful practice.

When he got back home from his trip to Calcutta, William found a letter waiting for him from the missionary society committee. Two more missionaries were on their way to India! With this news, William knew it was time to make a move. As the years had rolled by, it had become clear that the indigo dye factory in Mudnabatti had been built in the wrong place. The Tangan River flooded much too often, flooding the factory in the process. As a result, the business was not as profitable as it could or should be. While it was able to support William and his family and John Fountain, it would not financially support an entire community of missionaries.

For some time, William had been admiring a small indigo-dye factory at Kidderpore, twelve miles farther up the Tangan River. There the river didn't flood as often, and the main house had a large area of flat land around it where more houses and a workshop could easily be built. Upon hearing that new missionaries would be arriving, William decided to buy the factory.

It was a bold move, but one that had many advantages. William's oldest son, Felix, was now fourteen years old, and William wanted him to learn how to work hard and to help oversee the factory. Buying the factory would also provide a permanent base and steady income for the coming missionaries. William made a down payment on the factory with the money he had saved as overseer in Mudnabatti. Then he began the job of supervising the building of more houses and a printshop for the printing press.

Finally, on October 27, 1799, William sent John Fountain to Calcutta to await the arrival of the two missionaries from England. The letter from the committee had said to expect them about this time, though no mention had been made of exactly which ship they would be traveling on.

Two weeks later, William received a note and a newspaper article from John Fountain. The note said that John was headed for Serampore, and the newspaper article, cut from the front page of the *Calcutta Gazette,* told the rest of the story. Its headline blazed "Papist Missionaries Told to Go Home."

It was quite a shock. The article was about the missionaries William had sent John to meet. The word *papist* meant Roman Catholic; and to the British in India at that time, Roman Catholic meant French; and French meant spies! Somehow, the reporter had confused papist for Baptist. William read on and discovered that the missionaries had fled to Serampore, the Danish settlement fourteen miles north of Calcutta on the Hooghly River. The captain of the *Criterion,* the American ship that had transported the missionaries, was being held responsible for transporting unlicensed persons, possibly even spies, to India. Unless he handed them over to the British authorities or promised to return them to England, his ship would not be allowed to unload or reload cargo in India.

As if that were not enough, the newspaper reported that the missionary party consisted of eight adults and five children! *Could all of them have been sent to work with him?* William wondered. From Mudnabatti, there was little he could immediately do except pray and wait to hear more news from John Fountain.

Two weeks later, John arrived back in Mudnabatti with none other than William Ward, the young printer William had met and prayed with in Hull during his speaking tour of England six years before. William Ward had been given a temporary Danish visa by Colonel Bie, the governor of Semaphore. The visa had allowed him to travel unhindered through British territory.

As the three men talked, William learned that there were indeed eight adults and five children in the group, and not two people, as the missionary society committee had said. The group that set out from England consisted of William Grant, his wife, and their two children; Daniel Brunsdon and his wife; Joshua Marshman, his wife Hannah, and their three children; William Ward; and a Miss Mary Tidd. Tragically, soon after making it to Serampore, William Grant had become violently ill and had died, probably from typhoid fever, a common illness in the region. There was also some good news to report, at least as far as John Fountain was concerned. Mary Tidd was the fiancé John had left behind in England. A week after her arrival, she and John were married in Serampore.

As the men talked on, the rest of the story came tumbling out. Despite William's letters pleading that all missionaries coming to India get permits ahead of time, which would allow them to be his assistants in the indigo dye factory, the new recruits had decided to declare their occupation as Baptist missionaries. They didn't seem to grasp William's warning of just how unwelcome official missionaries were in India. Nor had they considered the difficult position they'd put the captain of the *Criterion* in when they disembarked his ship before the East India Company officials boarded it to arrest them.

After fleeing the ship, the group had hired a small boat to take them upriver to the Danish settlement of Serampore, where they were now all staying in a boardinghouse. They had also visited the Danish governor of the settlement. Governor Bie was an active Christian, and he welcomed them warmly, but he held out little hope that he could help them get permits to live in British India. Instead, he had offered them visas to live in Serampore under Danish protection.

Once the story was out, William wrote letters to everyone he knew of importance in Calcutta, but nobody could help the group. The message was clear: The East India Company did not want missionaries interfering in their territory. Period. However, after realizing that the group was made up of English Baptists and not French Papists, as reported in the newspaper, and that the group had escaped to Serampore, where it was out of the reach of the captain of the *Criterion,* the captain was allowed to unload his cargo and take on a new cargo of cotton.

All of this left William with a difficult decision to make. Should he finish the move to Kidderpore and the new indigo-dye factory, or should he go to

Serampore, where Colonel Bie had given the missionaries permission to live and work under Danish protection?

William had good reasons for continuing with the move to Kidderpore. He had just invested all the money he had in the place. He had also already moved his family into their new home there and had set up the printing press. And he knew that the factory should produce enough indigo dye to more than adequately provide financially for his family and the growing mission work. And then there were the many people in the area who had given generously to help open mission schools throughout the Dinadjpur area. And even though there were not yet any Christian converts, many people had heard the gospel message preached, and William hoped for a breakthrough soon. And how could he give up his permit to work, knowing he would not be granted another one? Where would the money come from for them all to live if he couldn't work?

On the other hand, it was time to get the Bengali translation of the Bible printed and out to the people. To do it, he needed a printer, and William Ward was stuck in Serampore. Besides, the missionary society committee had sent out thirteen people expecting him to be their leader. But how could he do that effectively if he was nearly two hundred miles away from them?

It took two days for William to come to a decision to make the move to Serampore. But would it be the right decision?

Chapter 13

# Sitting Together with the Missionaries

William Carey stepped off the boat onto the western bank of the Hooghly River. The red and white flag of Denmark flapped lightly in the breeze on a nearby flagstaff. There to meet him were two of the new missionaries: thirty-one-year-old Joshua Marshman, a schoolteacher from Bristol, and twenty-one-year-old Daniel Brunsdon. The men greeted each other warmly.

William was anxious to begin missionary work in Serampore. The first thing they needed was a place to live, and after seeing how expensive it was to rent houses, the group decided to buy a huge house on two acres of land located right beside the river. The house cost all the money the missionaries had brought with them from England, and the missionaries had to borrow a little more as well. While he didn't like to borrow money, William felt that purchasing the house and land would save them a lot of money in the end.

Within a week, all ten adults and nine children had moved into the house, which had enough room for each family to have two bedrooms plus a meeting hall, a printing room, a dining room, and a schoolroom.

The adults held many meetings to discuss how to run their missionary community. Although William had been in India the longest, he listened carefully to everyone's ideas. In the end, it was decided that each adult should take a month-long turn running the household. All the money that came into the community, whether from the missionary society committee, the proceeds from selling books, or fees from the school they planned to open, was to go into a group fund. No one would keep anything he earned for himself. Each person would be given a small monthly allowance.

William knew that in any community there would be disagreements and arguments, so he suggested they set aside Saturday nights to meet as a group and discuss any problems they might be having. He made each person promise to talk things out and forgive one another instead of holding a grudge.

Everyone was eager to get to work. William Ward unloaded the printing press from Kidderpore and gave it his seal of approval. The press was an older model, but it had been well looked after. William Ward housed it in a small outside room and the next day began handsetting the type for the Bengali edition of the Bible. He didn't work alone, however. Felix and William Carey Jr. were both fascinated by the press and the whole printing process, and they eagerly ran errands and did whatever William Ward asked them to.

William Carey and John Fountain, the only two of the missionaries who could speak Bengali, went out to preach each day in the surrounding suburbs. By now, William knew just the right way to start up a conversation with an Indian. The trick was to grab the person's attention with a question. "What is that mark you have on your face?" he would ask a Brahmin who had a painted white mark on his forehead.

"It is the mark of Telak," the Brahmin would reply proudly, not knowing that the Englishman he was talking to knew a great deal about their culture.

"And why do you wear it?" William would continue.

"It is the way we worship our gods. Only the most holy can wear it. The shastras tell us it is good."

William would nod, knowing that the shastras were the Brahmin holy books. Then he would pull a Bible from his bag. "Have you ever seen the Christian shastras?" he would ask. "It tells the story of one who is Lord of all creation."

From there, William would tell the person about the gospel message and challenge him to read the Bible he was holding. By asking questions like this, William was able to tell many people about the gospel. And many people were interested in what he had to say, yet there were still no converts!

Joshua Marshman lost no time getting started on his project. It had been decided that he should run a boarding school for boys and girls in the house. He placed an advertisement for the school in the *Calcutta Gazette* and soon had more than enough students. Employees of the East India Company were more than happy to send their sons and daughters to the school instead of having them make the dangerous voyage back to England to get a good education. The school taught the basic subjects, such as reading, writing, arithmetic, bookkeeping, and geography, and offered classes in Latin, Greek, Hebrew, Persian, and Sanskrit.

Hannah Marshman was a very capable woman, and everyone soon realized that, unlike Dolly Carey, she was every bit as much a missionary as her husband. She worked alongside him and ran the girls' side of the boarding school. She also took control of the two younger Carey boys, Jabez and Jonathan, who often ran wild around the house. Dolly had lapsed back into her unstable mental condition and hardly ever left her room or took care of the boys, and William just didn't seem to notice when they got out of control.

Joshua and Hannah Marshman did the work of six missionaries, and within a month of opening the school, they opened a second one for Indian boys. The classes were to be taught in Bengali. Within a week, forty boys were enrolled.

Of course, William was delighted by it all. Things were finally beginning to fall into place. William had something positive to put in his reports to the missionary society committee. Yes, the days were long and hard, but the missionaries were beginning to see the results of their work.

Two months after arriving in Serampore, William learned just how right his decision had been to move there instead of going to Kidderpore. George Udney had returned to England and had been replaced by another commercial resident, who was completely opposed to the work of missionaries in India. George Udney's replacement forbade any missionary from preaching in the villages of the district. Had William still been there, he would not have been allowed to continue with his missionary work. At the same time, Lord Wellesley, the governor-general of British India had been angered by some things printed in the newspaper and had issued an order banning all printing presses outside of Calcutta. Again, had William stayed in Kidderpore, his printing press would surely have been confiscated. Instead, it was safely in Serampore and ready to start printing the Bible in Bengali.

Realizing that printing the Bible in four volumes was a huge task, William Ward came up with a novel idea. Why not start with the Gospels and print them one at a time? His idea proved to be a success. William Ward was able to print the Gospels much faster and more cheaply than a four-volume Bible, and soon hundreds of copies of the Gospel of Matthew were being given away.

It wasn't long before they had to hire some Indian workers to help with the press. Soon, the printshop had a typesetter, five pressmen, a folder, and a binder, as well as William Ward, Daniel Brunsdon, and Felix and William Jr., all working full time. The twelve of them printed six thousand half-sheets a week, more than William Ward had thought was humanly possible!

However, paying the Indian workers, not to mention buying paper and ink supplies, took a lot of money. Soon the mission ran out of funds for printing. William Ward came up with another bold idea. William Carey had told them all that there were many men in the East India Company who secretly cheered on their missionary work. William Ward thus wondered, Why not ask them to help? That's exactly what they did. The mission placed an advertisement in the *Calcutta Gazette* asking readers to take out a subscription to help with the printing. For four pounds, a subscriber would eventually get a single printed copy of the Bible in Bengali, with the balance of the money going toward printing more Bibles. The subscription idea was a huge success, and enough money was raised to keep the printing press operating.

When the governor-general read the ad in the newspaper, he was outraged. Hadn't he banned all printing presses from the Bengal district except for Calcutta? So why did these English people have a printing press in Serampore? He ordered the Reverend Brown, the army chaplain at Fort William, to visit him immediately to discuss the situation.

The Reverend Brown was the same person who, seven years earlier, had slammed the door in

William Carey's face and refused to help William and his family soon after they'd arrived in India. William was not a man to hold a grudge, however, and he had promised himself that day seven years earlier that he would not be bitter at the chaplain. True to his word, soon after moving to Serampore, he had visited the Reverend Brown. As a result, the two men had become good friends, and William visited the chaplain often to keep him up-to-date on the mission work in Serampore. The Reverend Brown was thus able to assure the governor-general that William and his group intended to print only Bibles on their printing press and nothing that would criticize the British government or the East India Company. Upon hearing this, the governor-general calmed down. Indeed, from then on, he began to take a positive interest in what William was up to.

By 1800, the missionary society had sent out seven men, accompanied by their families, as missionaries to India. By August of that year, only five of the men were still with the mission. William Grant had died twenty-two days after arriving in India, and Dr. Thomas had left the mission and his indigo dye factory and gone farther inland, where he had become involved in the lucrative business of distilling rum. And they were about to lose another one of their number. John Fountain had taken a trip up the river to quietly visit some of the villages in and around Mudnabatti, where he had once been a regular visitor. While there, he became ill with dysentery and died. He and Mary had been married for only nine months. Several months later, William Ward married Mary Fountain.

October 1800 marked seven years in India for the Carey family. Things had been desperate and difficult in the beginning, especially during the first year. But now William felt that things were finally going well for him. He spoke fluent Bengali and Sanskrit and had a team of fellow missionaries around him. Together they ran a successful English school and another for Indian children and had a printing press busily turning out dozens of copies of the Scriptures in Bengali.

Just one thing was lacking—there were still no converts. With no conversions to show for their efforts, William secretly worried that the missionary society back in England might become discouraged and stop sending more missionaries, money, and supplies. But that was about to change. A Serampore carpenter named Krishna Pal was taking his children down to the Hooghly River to bathe. As he did so, he slipped on the top step of the stairs leading down into the water, fell, and dislocated his shoulder. Since he was not far from the mission house, he sent his oldest child there to get help. Dr. Thomas happened to be visiting the house, and when he heard what had happened, he rounded up William and Joshua Marshman to help. Together the men rushed to the scene of the accident to help Krishna Pal. This "help" involved tying him to a tree to keep him still so that Dr. Thomas could jerk his shoulder back into place!

While Krishna Pal sat under the tree recovering from his ordeal, Dr. Thomas shared with him the gospel message. Krishna Pal listened politely, as so many other Hindus had, but said nothing. The next day, William visited Krishna Pal to see how his shoulder was and to invite him to visit the mission house. Later that day, Krishna Pal came to the house with a friend, Gokul. The two men came the following day, and the day after that, too. In fact, long after his shoulder had healed, Krishna Pal and Gokul continued to visit the mission house to talk to the missionaries about their God.

Finally, three days before Christmas, 1800, both Krishna Pal and Gokul announced they wanted to become Christians. It was a wonderful day for William. At last, after seven years of work, there were two Indian converts.

The real question, though, in all the missionaries' minds was, would an Indian, even one who had believed the gospel message, have the courage to break caste? The question was answered when Dr. Thomas, who was still visiting at the house, invited Krishna Pal and Gokul to eat lunch with the missionaries. Normally, this would have been impossible. A Hindu would be breaking caste by eating with a non-Hindu. Amazingly, the two men willingly sat down and ate with their new friends.

The Indian servants at the mission house were shocked, and news quickly spread that two Hindus were sitting together with the missionaries. By the time the two of them left the mission house that afternoon, it seemed that everyone in Serampore knew what they had done. Many Hindus were furious. How dare two of their own break caste? People waited in the street outside their homes to throw rocks at the two men as they hurried by. When Gokul finally made it home, he found his wife Kamal and his mother packing their bags. The women had heard the terrible news and were so humiliated they could not stay a minute longer in the same house with him.

Krishna Pal's wife Rasoo and his four daughters did stay, but they were very scared. They feared they would all be killed by the angry mob that had gathered outside their home.

The next day, Krishna Pal, Rasoo, and their oldest daughter were thrown into prison. When his oldest daughter had been only six years old, Krishna Pal had arranged for her to be married to a boy in Calcutta. The daughter had not yet met the boy, but that didn't matter. By Hindu custom, the "marriage" was official anyway. Within twenty-four hours, news of the two Christian converts in Serampore had spread to Calcutta, where the father of the boy who was arranged to marry Krishna Pal's daughter had heard it and become enraged. If the daughter stayed in the same house as her Christian convert father, she would no longer be fit to marry. So the boy's father went straightaway to fetch his son's bride.

By the time the father arrived in Serampore, Krishna Pal had talked to his family about his conversion, and they, too, were seriously considering becoming Christians. As a result, his daughter was not sure she wanted to marry a Hindu, and of course, Krishna Pal would not make her. When the bridegroom's father heard this, he stirred up the crowd still gathered outside the house from the night before. The crowd dragged Krishna Pal, his wife, and his daughter before a judge, who had them imprisoned for breaking a marriage contract.

As soon as they heard about this, William and Joshua Marshman hurried to Governor Bie to ask for help. The governor ordered the three prisoners released from jail while the whole matter was looked into.

While in jail, both Krishna Pal's daughter and his wife, Rasoo, decided to become Christians, as did his other three daughters later that night. William greeted the news enthusiastically. Now there were seven Hindu Christians in the Bengal region.

On December 28, 1800, a baptismal service was held. All seven of the new converts had agreed to be baptized. However, when they saw the huge crowd of Hindus and English people waiting on the steps of the Hooghly River to watch the ceremony, six of them became too scared to continue. They feared they might be killed if the crowd became angry.

In the end, William Carey baptized Krishna Pal and his own son Felix that day. He explained the service in English when he baptized Felix and in Bengali when he baptized Krishna Pal. Then they sang a hymn in English and another hymn, which Ram Boshu had written, in Bengali.

As Felix and Krishna Pal stepped from the water of the Hooghly River after their baptisms, many European men and women were there to welcome them as Christian brothers. Among them was Governor Bie, who was moved to tears as he shook Krishna Pal's hand.

Another person in the group was Charlotte Rumohr, who lived in the large house next to the mission. Charlotte Rumohr was a wealthy, well-educated countess from Denmark. She was an invalid and had come to India in the hopes that the warm climate would improve her health. Charlotte Rumohr had never had any time for religion until she started taking private English lessons from William Carey. As she had learned about the work William and the others in his group were involved in, she had become fascinated and was soon drawn into the activities of the mission house.

As he drifted off to sleep that night, his head still brimming with the day's activities, William Carey began to think about what lay ahead for the mission. He was sure that now that they had their first converts, things around the mission house were going to become more hectic than ever. Indeed, big changes lay ahead.

Chapter 14

# Professor

March 5, 1801, was a day no one at the Serampore mission house would forget. As individual Gospels had been typeset, they had been printed as single volumes; but this day, the first complete New Testament in Bengali rolled off the printing press. The beautiful black, leather-bound book was placed on the communion table in the chapel, and the entire community gathered to offer prayers of thanks for it.

No one was more thankful than William Carey. The New Testament represented eight years of his labor, not to mention fifteen months of labor by the team of printers and binders who worked under William Ward in the printshop. Although it was a wonderful day of celebration, no one in the chapel had any idea the role that the Bengali New Testament would play in saving the mission.

Far away on the other side of the world, Europe was in an uproar. The war between the English and the French had been dragging on for years. In addition, French leader Napoleon Bonaparte had led his army to victory over a number of European countries. Frustrated at what was happening in Europe, and by their ships continually being attacked, the British had claimed the right to search all ships at sea to look for pirates and privateers. Russia, Sweden, Prussia, and Denmark had joined forces to form an alliance called the Armed Neutrality of the North to resist British attempts to search their ships. The British, however, were convinced the Armed Neutrality of the North was plotting with the French to destroy their navy. Tensions between the two sides steadily grew.

In India, however, news of such events was slow in coming, and things continued as usual. As soon as more Bengali New Testaments were bound, William would send a copy to each person who had subscribed to the work of the printshop and to other important people who had taken an interest in the work of the mission. A copy was sent to the king of Denmark with a letter thanking him for his protection in Serampore. Another copy was sent to King George III of England, and yet another copy to the Reverend Brown in Calcutta. It was this particular copy of the New Testament that was used to save the work of the mission.

In Calcutta, changes had been taking place. The governor-general, Lord Wellesley, was an intelligent man who had become very concerned about the young clerks being sent to India from England. These clerks were the sons of wealthy English families, but they were being sent out as young as fifteen years of age, usually before they'd had a chance to start, let alone finish, university.

Once these young clerks arrived in India, they were given jobs that took only a few hours a day to complete. They were paid well for their labor and had servants to cook, clean, and keep house for them. As a result, they tended to become very lazy, since there was little left for them to do in their spare time but engage in horse racing, gambling, drinking parties, and secret meetings with Indian women. These young clerks were also promoted regularly as the men over them either retired and returned to England or died from tropical diseases. In time, a fifteen-year-old clerk could be promoted to a judge or other high-ranking official, even though he had no special training for such a position. The young men had little understanding of the culture and language of the people they were ruling over, and this led to many misunderstandings.

Lord Wellesley had a solution to the problem. He suggested that instead of starting work upon their arrival in India, the clerks go to college for two years. During this time, they would learn the history and geography of India as well as the country's culture and several of its languages. Not only would the new clerks have a chance to "grow up," but the college professors would have a chance to get to know the young clerks and could recommend for important jobs those who they thought had the most potential. It seemed like a great idea, except to the directors of the East India Company. The directors argued against the college. Not only would it cost them money, but they could see no point in worrying whether the Indian people were happy with their English overlords. What mattered was trade.

Lord Wellesley argued that it did matter. Those who were rude and lazy as clerks were even more rude and lazy as they gained power; and in the end, such leaders would cause the Indians to rebel. Thus, Lord Wellesley used his power as governor-general and ordered a college for clerks to be established.

In 1800, Fort William College opened with the Reverend Brown as its provost (principal). The new college was modeled after Oxford and Cambridge universities in England and had one hundred young Englishmen from Calcutta, Bombay, and Madras enrolled.

When the college was opened, Lord Wellesley was not aware of a single European in all of India who knew enough Bengali or Sanskrit to teach the new clerks. However, the Reverend Brown showed him the copy of the Bengali New Testament he had received from William Carey. As the governor-general thumbed through its pages, the two men talked and agreed that perhaps there was one European in India capable of teaching these languages after all.

William Carey read the letter that had been hand-delivered to him by a servant of the Reverend Brown. "Me, a lecturer at Fort William College!" he said aloud to himself before bursting into laughter. Then he added, "The Reverend Mr. Brown must have forgotten I've never been to college myself. As soon as I remind him, he'll know I'm not the man he is looking for."

William's education had consisted of attending the church school his father ran, and then only until he was twelve years old. From that time on, he had worked and never had another day of formal education. Yes, he was an ordained minister, but while Anglican ministers like the Reverend Brown had to go to college to be ordained, Baptist ministers did not.

Not wanting to seem ungrateful for the invitation, William decided to row one of the mission boats down to Calcutta and explain the misunderstanding to the Reverend Brown in person. When he arrived, he was surprised to find that the Reverend Brown already knew that he had no formal education other than his time attending the church school in Paulerspury. The Reverend Brown told William that he was the one man in India who knew the customs and the language of the people well enough to teach them to others. Many other Europeans had been in India much longer than he had, but they had lived in the pampered world of servants and upper-class English society and had little idea of, or interest in, the Indian people. William, on the other hand, spoke their language, read their literature, and knew how to talk meaningfully with the people. Given this, the Reverend Brown was convinced that William was the man to teach Bengali and Sanskrit at the new college. William, though, was not so sure, but he promised to talk to his fellow missionaries about the invitation.

"What a wonderful opportunity," announced Joshua Marshman when William told him about his visit with the Reverend Brown.

Finally, after several days of thought and prayer, William decided to accept the invitation. The man who had left school at age twelve was about to take charge of the Language Department at Fort William College!

William Carey's acceptance of the position happened just in the nick of time, because four days later, in the middle of the night on May 8, 1801, British troops crept into Serampore and captured it without a single shot being fired. The next morning, all Europeans in Serampore were summoned to King's House and informed that news had just reached India that the British navy under Admiral Nelson had fought and defeated the Danish fleet at the Battle of Copenhagen. (The battle actually occurred in April, but it took a month for the news to travel overland to India.) Britain and Denmark were officially at war with each other, and as part of the war, Serampore had been captured and occupied. The Danish flag was lowered and the Union Jack hoisted in its place. Serampore was officially declared British territory, and the Danish governor was jailed as a prisoner of war.

It had been only eighteen months since the missionaries had fled to Serampore to avoid being arrested by the British and returned to England. Now because of a war in Europe, they were once again living in British territory. They had no more protection from being arrested and deported to England, except for one thing: The leader of their mission was the newest appointee to the staff of Fort William College, Lord Wellesley's pet project. To their surprise, there was no longer any talk about rounding up the missionaries and sending them home. As long as William taught at the college, they were all welcome to stay in India!

Even though he was the head of the Language Department at the college, William was given the title of tutor. Since it was a government position and he did not belong to the Church of England, he could not be given the title professor. The job did come with some benefits, however. William had a room to live in, free food from the dining room, and a salary of five hundred rupees, or about sixty-five pounds, per month.

When the Serampore mission house was first opened, it had been agreed that all the money each person earned would go into a common account. William gladly turned over to the group the money he earned. Much of it was spent buying paper and employing more Indians to assist William Ward and Felix in the print shop.

Soon William had developed a routine that suited him well. On Monday evening, just before the sun set, he would row down the river to Calcutta. He would stay there and teach until Friday evening, when he would row back up the river to see his family and spend time preaching in Serampore. While he was away during the week, William Ward watched over the two older Carey boys. Felix was William Ward's full-time printing assistant, and thirteen-year-old William Jr. worked after school in the Bindery Department. Eight-year-old Jabez and five-year-old Jonathan were under the firm but kind care of Hannah Marshman, who also watched over Dolly Carey when William was gone. By now, Dolly was completely deranged and had to be confined to her room.

The war between Britain and Denmark was soon over, and six months after they had captured it, the British handed Serampore back to the Danish government.

At the same time, the mission continued to grow. Krishna Pal's wife and daughters found the courage to be baptized, as did Gokul's wife. Thousands of gospel tracts were printed and given away, and many Hindus who did not feel comfortable talking to Europeans, silently made their way to Krishna Pal's home in the late evening to talk to him about Christianity.

There were some sad times in the mission too. In July 1801, Daniel Brunsdon died following a short illness, and just three months later, Dr. Thomas died. William mourned both deaths. Although Dr.

Thomas had been difficult to work with, he had been the one who inspired William to go to India, and he had also played a vital role in winning their first Hindu converts to Christianity. Despite his erratic behavior, Dr. Thomas had been loyal to the end and generous to the mission, though he did leave behind a lot of debt!

William worried. There was so much to do, and now so few missionaries to do it. He tried to think of a way to have a "backup" for each of the remaining missionaries. That way, if one of the other missionaries died suddenly, the backup person could step in and take over his responsibilities. But William needn't have worried. The three surviving men, William Ward, Joshua Marshman, and William Carey himself, would all remain in excellent health for the next twenty-three years! The men worked together so well that they became known in Europe and North America as the "Serampore Triad."

By the end of 1801, more Hindus had been converted, the group enjoyed the protection of the British and Danish flags, copies of the Bengali New Testament were continuing to roll off the press, the missionary community was stable, and William had a job that allowed him to meet with some of the most powerful people in India. And of course, he always used such meetings to push for the spread of the gospel message throughout India.

One of the men William got to know well through his new position was Lord Wellesley. As governor-general, Lord Wellesley took his responsibility to rule British India seriously. For some time, he had been considering the practice of sati. The question was whether he should ban the practice altogether? Many high-caste Hindus told him that their sacred writings demanded that a widow die beside her husband. Others, though, told him privately that the shastras did not say that at all. Because Lord Wellesley didn't know whom to believe, he turned to the one man he knew he could trust to give him an honest and complete answer—William Carey.

William spent many months researching the practice of sati, and in the end came to the conclusion that while it was suggested in the shastras, it was never actually commanded that a widow be burned with her dead husband. He gave his report to the governor-general and added a report on another practice that had bothered him for a long time—infanticide. In particular, the practice was carried out on the island of Saugor, in the mouth of the Ganges River, where live babies were thrown into the river to be devoured by crocodiles as a form of human sacrifice. William hoped that Lord Wellesley would act to outlaw both sati and infanticide.

The governor-general studied both reports closely, and in 1802, he issued a law banning infanticide. When it came to sati, however, he was under mounting pressure from Hindus not to ban the practice. So while he disagreed with it, he allowed it to continue.

Meanwhile, William's reputation as a teacher grew each year. In 1806, the rules of the college were changed so that the title of professor could be bestowed on him. His salary was doubled to go along with the new title!

The next year, 1807, was mostly a happy one for William. His son William Jr. became an ordained Baptist minister. William Jr. married and moved upriver to Malda to be a missionary to the workers involved in the indigo dye industry. As the year drew to a close, though, there was sadness. On December 7, Dolly Carey died after a short illness. Most outsiders thought that William would be secretly relieved, since she had been such a burden to him for so long. But William grieved for her. He had always loved his wife. When people had urged him to put Dolly in an institution for insane people, he'd always refused, saying that no matter what happened, she was his wife and the mother of his children and he would keep her with him till the end.

Because Dolly Carey had been such a burden to her husband, there was a lot of concern six months later when William announced that he and Charlotte Rumohr were to be married. Charlotte was the Danish countess who lived in the house next door and who had taken an active interest in the work of the mission since the early days when Krishna Pal had been baptized.

Everyone in the community loved Charlotte, a bright and kind woman. There was just one problem: She was partially crippled. When she was fifteen years old, the castle where she lived with her family had caught on fire. Charlotte had awakened to find her bedchamber filled with smoke. Instead of escaping the fire, she had run through the flames to awaken her parents. As a result, everyone escaped alive, but Charlotte's legs had been so badly burned she was not able to walk much after that. Her lungs had also been damaged by the smoke, and sometimes she found it difficult to talk.

Despite people's concerns that Charlotte would be another burden on him, William went ahead with the wedding. Lady Charlotte Emelia Rumohr became the second Mrs. Carey. The two were very happy together. Charlotte had a mind that was as brilliant as William's, and she spoke seven languages herself. She was a great help to her new husband in his translation work.

Charlotte helped the mission in other ways. She donated her house to the mission school and rented out another of her properties to support Indian preachers who were being sent out from Serampore into the surrounding countryside to spread the gospel message. Although she spent much of her day lying on a couch, she took an active interest in all that was going on around her. William often turned to her for advice and comfort, something he would need a lot of very soon.

Chapter 15

# Rebuild and Replace

March 11, 1812, found William Carey eating lunch with several of his assistants at Fort William College. Between mouthfuls, the men discussed the new multilanguage dictionary that was being typeset and prepared for printing back in Serampore. Many of the assistants eating lunch with William had helped on the project, which had taken five years to complete. The dictionary gave a word in Sanskrit and then its translation in every language in Asia. Even though it had been time consuming to prepare, William knew it was a resource that would make all future translation work much easier.

The bell on the college clock tower had just chimed one o'clock when Joshua Marshman burst into the room where the group was eating. William turned to him with a surprised look on his face, wondering what he was doing in Calcutta.

"I have to speak to you," Joshua Marshman said in an urgent voice.

The serious look on Joshua's face caused William to get up quickly and lead Joshua to his office. Seated in the office, Joshua Marshman told William his reason for coming. "It's the print shop," he began. "Last night a fire swept through it, and there's nothing left."

William's mouth dropped open. Stunned, he sat in silence for a moment, absorbing what he had just heard. Then finally he uttered, "Nothing left? What do you mean, nothing left?"

"It started in the paper storeroom. William Ward had stayed after the workers had gone home. He was sitting in his office when he smelled smoke. He turned and saw it seeping in under the door. He ran down the corridor, with the smoke getting thicker all the time, until he couldn't go any farther. He could hear the flames crackling in the storeroom."

William placed his elbows on the edge of his desk, leaned forward, cupped his head in his hands, and let out a deep sigh.

Joshua Marshman continued. "William Ward knew the fire was too big for him to fight alone, so he ran back through the building, closing all the windows and doors as he went. He raced outside yelling. A few of the workers were still milling around outside, and they ran for buckets of water. I was in the schoolroom and raced outside. By then, smoke was billowing from the roof. That's when I saw William Ward running back from the toolshed with a saw. He yelled for me to climb onto the roof with him. He sawed a hole right where he thought the fire had started, and then buckets of water were hoisted up, and we poured them down onto the fire. It took four hours to put it out, and even then some of the paper was still smoldering."

Joshua Marshman shifted position in his chair, and as he did so, William noticed how tired he looked. Joshua had rings under his eyes. Then William thought about what Joshua had just told him. "So the fire destroyed only the paper? Thank God the translations and typefaces are safe. What would we have done if we had lost them?"

Joshua Marshman hung his head. Large tears rolled down his cheeks onto his shirt. "We did lose everything," he said.

"But..." William's voice trailed off. He could think of nothing to say.

When Joshua Marshman regained his composure, he continued with the story. "After the fire had died down, William Ward and I left. He had some papers he wanted to move out of his office just in case there was any looting during the night. I took the schoolboys back to their dormitory. They had been helping fight the fire, and it was well past their bedtime.

"No one is quite sure who did it, but while we were away, somebody opened all the doors and windows in the print shop. With a tremendous whoosh, the fire leapt back to life and spread quickly. By the time William Ward and I got back, the whole building was well ablaze, and the wind had picked up, fanning the flames and sending sparks onto the school buildings. I got the children up again, and about a hundred of us formed bucket lines to get water to the fire, but it wasn't much help. Finally, about two o'clock this morning, the fire burned itself out. But the damage is done. The whole print shop and everything in it is ruined."

"I must see what can be done," said William, after a long silence. "You wait here while I tell the provost what has happened and ask to be released from my lectures."

An hour later they were rowing back up the Hooghly River toward Serampore. The Reverend Thomason, the college chaplain, had been sent with the two missionaries to help in any way he could.

The scene that greeted William as he stepped from the boat was dreadful beyond words. Where the print shop had stood there was now a tangle of charred wood mixed with pieces of twisted iron and clumps of still smoldering paper. Thin pillars of smoke rose into the air. Everyone stopped what he was doing as William walked silently around the charred remains. As he walked, William wept quietly. Then he turned to Joshua Marshman and said, "In one short evening, the labors of years are consumed. How unsearchable are the ways of God!"

William Ward came out of the mission house to greet William.

"Was nothing saved?" William asked him.

"The news is better than we first thought," he replied. "The press itself survived the fire and, with a little work, can be made to print again. And there are about four thousand letters of typeface unharmed. Some of the paper in the middle of the stacks is also still usable."

"But the manuscripts?" William asked in a whisper, knowing in his heart what the answer would be.

"The manuscripts are all burned. I am so sorry," replied William Ward, taking William Carey gently by the arm. "Come inside. Charlotte is anxious to see you." He steered William Carey away from the destruction and into the house. Inside, William's wife was lying on the couch, as she often was. When she saw William, she reached for his hand. William sat on the floor beside her, and together they wept.

That evening, William and the missionaries met to go over all that had been lost in the fire: the final draft of the multilanguage dictionary, the Sikh and Telugu grammars, ten versions of the Bible that were in various stages of being printed, a translation and interpretation of Hindu religious writing that William and Joshua Marshman had been working on for over six years, many sets of hand-cut type fonts in various Asian languages, and hundreds of reams of paper.

"All in all," William told his fellow missionaries, "I estimate between nine and ten thousand pounds worth of goods went up in flames last night." (Of course, there was no way to put a price on the manuscripts of the various translations William had completed, which had been in the print shop waiting to be printed.) "However," he continued, "we must not let this bring us down. We must stay the course, trusting God, who had brought us safe thus far. We can rebuild and replace what has been lost."

It took four days before the remains of the print shop were cool enough to search thoroughly. Each fragment of paper was carefully brought to William to be identified. Some pieces were pages from his translations. William gently laid these pages in boxes to be recopied later.

As they combed through the remains, they were not able to determine what had caused the fire. Nor were they able to find out who had opened the doors and windows in the print shop, allowing the fire to be fanned back to life.

The Indian servants were surprised by how quickly the missionaries started to rebuild. They had assumed the missionaries would simply pack up and leave after the fire.

News of the disaster quickly spread throughout the district. Help began to pour in. William's students at the college took up a collection for him. George Udney, who had originally donated the printing press, was again living in India, and he also made a donation. Altogether, this money amounted to almost nine hundred pounds.

It took six months for news of the fire to reach Great Britain, but when it did, Christians there sprung into action. William Carey and the printing press were the topic of conversation and prayer in nearly every church in the nation. It was the first time many people in England had heard of William, and what they heard interested them. Individuals and churches gave what they could toward rebuilding the print shop. The Baptist church in Moulton, where William had been pastor, gave fifty pounds, while churches in Edinburgh banded together to raised eight hundred pounds. William Wilberforce, the antislavery campaigner, sent ten pounds, and the Bible Society, which had been formed in 1804, donated two thousand reams of paper.

Within two months of news of the fire reaching England, ten thousand pounds had been collected, much of it coming from Anglican churches as well as Baptist and other denominations. By Christmas, Andrew Fuller had to send out letters on behalf of the missionary society telling people that enough money had been collected to replace everything destroyed by the fire and that they need not send any more.

Everywhere members of the missionary society committee went in England, they were asked to show a portrait of William Carey. People had heard so much about him, but they wanted to see what he looked like. However, there was no portrait of William. So Andrew Fuller wrote to William Ward and asked him to arrange for one to be painted. William Ward contacted Robert Home, supposedly the best artist in Asia, and with reluctance, William posed while his picture was painted. He chose to be painted sitting at a desk, surrounded by papers and books, with an assistant at his side and a Sanskrit translation in his hand.

William Ward had the portrait sent back to England, where engravings of it were made. The committee then sold the engravings for one pound each. The profit from sales went to the missionaries in the Serampore mission.

Soon portraits of William Carey hung in churches and homes across Great Britain. It was a good thing William never found out how many engravings of himself had been sold. He would have been embarrassed to think that so many people wanted the picture of a bald, fifty-two-year-old missionary hanging in their parlor!

The fire in Serampore and subsequent fund-raising in Great Britain had another effect. People who had not cared about missionaries before now began to question the East India Company's policy of not allowing more missionaries into India. Indeed, while William Carey, William Ward, and Joshua Marshman had been in India for many years and had powerful friends there and in England, the East India Company was still officially opposed to missionaries. It had demonstrated this opposition over the years by refusing to allow into India a group of five families from North America who had come to join the Serampore mission and by deporting Dr. William Johns, who had come to India to work alongside the missionaries.

William Wilberforce, who had successfully campaigned to abolish slavery on British soil, led the fight against the East India Company. Everywhere he went, he spoke out for sending more missionaries to India. "Now that the slave trade is abolished, the exclusion of missionaries from India is by far the greatest of our national sins," was his battle cry.

Churches all over Great Britain joined the fight, and in 1813, William Wilberforce presented to Parliament a petition with over half a million signatures, all urging that more missionaries be allowed into India.

The petition led to a long debate in Parliament. Men who had been past governors-general of India were asked to testify. Lord Wellesley spoke up on behalf of missionaries, using all the good done by the Serampore Triad as evidence of the value of the work of missionaries. Other men tried to stir up suspicion and fear. What if missionaries ended up causing riots? they asked. Or what if they insulted the local religions and disturbed the peace? And worse, what if trade was interrupted as a result of their actions?

In the course of the debate, William Wilberforce gave a speech in which he described William Carey's contributions to literature, translation work, cultural understanding, horticulture, and agriculture. It seemed, however, to be the fact that William gave all of his fifteen-hundred-pound salary to the mission that really impressed the politicians! In the end, William Wilberforce won the day, and on June 28, 1813, the charter of the East India Company was amended to say that it was the duty of Britain to "promote the happiness of the Indian people" and that a part of doing this was to offer them "useful religious and moral teachings."

The way was finally open for missionaries to travel freely to and around India. William Carey received the news in the best way possible. His brother Tom's youngest son, Eustace, was the first person issued a license to be a missionary in India. Eustace arrived and presented himself to his uncle William for service.

Chapter 16

# Growing Pains

The act of Parliament that amended the charter of the East India Company and allowed for the free flow of missionaries into India brought many opportunities to the Serampore mission. For the first time, the governor-general was allowed to officially request missionary help. Within weeks of receiving notification of the new law, the governor-general at the time, Lord Moira, asked William to visit him to ask William for missionaries to be sent to the Moluccan island of Amboyna on the other side of the Bay of Bengal.

William rushed back to Serampore to share the good news and ask for a volunteer to go. To his surprise, his nineteen-year-old son, Jabez, took up the call. Within three days, Jabez was baptized, ordained as a Baptist minister, married, and ready to go! His brother Felix, himself married with three children, was visiting Serampore at the time and was able to participate in the service to commission Jabez for his new calling.

Felix knew what it was like to go out alone as a missionary. Several years earlier he had set out from Serampore and gone to Burma, where he had established his own mission station. He had his father's gift for languages and translated portions of the Bible into Burmese. He also compiled a dictionary of the Burmese language.

Before leaving for Burma, he had also become interested in medicine and had read about Edward Jenner's daring experiment in 1796 with the first smallpox vaccine. After he arrived in Burma, Felix became convinced that the Burmese people were likely to catch many deadly diseases as their contact with people from other places grew. He convinced the king of Burma to let him give smallpox vaccinations to the local people. At that time, this represented the most widespread use of a vaccine in the world. When it proved successful, Felix Carey became well-known in Burma.

Sadly, though, on the trip back to Burma after visiting Serampore, the boat in which Felix and his family were traveling capsized in a storm. Felix was the only one who made it to shore. The rest of his family were drowned. A printing press, copies of the Gospels in Burmese, and the only copy of his Burmese dictionary were also lost. The loss of his family sent Felix into deep depression, from which he took a long time to recover.

Soon after Eustace Carey's arrival in Serampore as the first licensed English missionary to India, more missionaries followed. This should have been a good thing, but it turned out not to be so. The new missionaries being sent by the Baptist Missionary Society, as the Particular Baptist Society for Propagating the Gospel was now called, were all young and did not know much about missionary work. Instead of quietly watching and listening to the older missionaries and following their advice, they soon began to hold private meetings among themselves to complain about and criticize the older missionaries' way of doing things. For William, this was heartbreaking, and more so when his nephew Eustance joined their meetings.

The new missionaries complained that Joshua Marshman was too bossy and expected them to obey him and that William Ward wanted them to work too hard. They wondered why William Carey dressed up and ate fabulous meals at the governor-general's mansion. Did he think he was better than everyone else in the mission? And why did the print shop at Serampore print schoolbooks that made no mention of religion in them? And what happened to all of the money the Baptist Missionary Society sent to Serampore?

They could have easily got the answers to their questions by simply asking the older missionaries, but they seemed more content to talk among themselves and stir up trouble.

When the original group of missionaries had settled in Serampore thirteen years before and established their community, they had set it up in such a way that every male missionary had one vote on important issues. Now that system worked against the longtime missionaries. After years of working in great agreement together, William Ward, Joshua Marshman, and William Carey found themselves outvoted on almost every decision concerning missionary work at Serampore. This was difficult for the three of them to accept, but they tried to be as gracious as possible. What was more difficult for them to accept was the fact that these new missionaries had also written letters to the missionary society complaining about them.

Finally, the community came to an uneasy peace that lasted for several years. However, in 1814, John Sutcliff died, followed a year later by Andrew Fuller. These two men, along with John Ryland, had been "holding the ropes" for William back in England throughout his time in India. They had been the core of the original missionary society committee. With the growth of the mission, they had been joined on the committee by nineteen new members. These new members were good friends of the young missionaries who had recently been sent out, but they had never met William Carey, Joshua Marshman, or William Ward.

Now with John Ryland left as the only person in the missionary society who had been directly involved in sending out William Carey, the new committee decided to find out whether the longtime missionaries in Serampore would follow its orders. It issued an order that all of the mission's property in Serampore, including the printing press, paper supplies, established churches and schools, and all houses and related buildings, be signed over to the committee in England so that it could take direct control over the property.

When William Carey, now fifty-five years old, read the order, he wrote immediately to the committee and announced that he had no intention of handing over the property. He argued, as he had in his book *Enquiry* twenty-four years before, that a mission cannot be successfully run from halfway around the world. For one thing, it took far too long to communicate problems and decisions back and forth to England. For another, the committee had little idea of the circumstances the missionaries faced in India. William also appealed desperately to John Ryland to try to make the rest of the committee be reasonable.

In 1816, John Ryland died. All three of the original "rope holders" were now gone. William also got more bad news about this time. His father, with whom he had kept in regular contact, had died. If William had ever been thinking about returning to England for a furlough, such thoughts were now gone. "Wherever I look," William wrote about England, "I see a blank. Were I to revisit that dear country, I should have an entirely new set of friendships to form."

Finally, in August 1817, the uneasy peace that had existed between the old and the new missionaries in

Serampore was shattered with the arrival of William Pearce and his wife.

William Pearce was an experienced printer and should have been a great help to William Ward. The problem was that the committee in England had sent William Pearce to India and had "ordered" him to stay in Serampore. Up until this time, the missionaries in Serampore had been the ones who made the final decision on where a new missionary should serve. As the years passed, a number of other mission stations had been established around India, and most new missionaries were sent on to help staff these stations. But this time, the committee had said where it wanted a new missionary to be stationed. Although this didn't seem like a major problem, especially since Pearce was a printer and the print shop was in Serampore, it showed William Carey, Joshua Marshman, and William Ward that the committee in England was challenging them for control of the mission in India.

The whole situation weighed heavily on William, who had come to India to do the peaceful work of sharing the gospel message, not to argue and squabble over who controlled the mission. At the same time, William was worried about Felix, who had become depressed and mentally unstable after the drowning of his family. The last time William had heard from him, he was wandering aimlessly in the state of Assam. On top of this, William's health was not good. William had been riding in a horse-drawn buggy when the horse had bolted. He had been forced to leap to safety, but in doing so, he had broken several bones in his foot. His foot had taken many months to heal, forcing him to have to be carried to and from Fort William College. Even after his foot finally did heal, William had a pronounced limp for the rest of his life.

By the end of 1817, the young missionaries and their families had left Serampore and, with the approval and support of the Baptist Missionary Society, had set up their own mission center fourteen miles downriver in Calcutta. There they established a mission identical to the mission in Serampore, complete with a printing press, church, school, and translation center. William would not have minded this so much had they gone to some other unevangelized part of India to set up their work, but establishing an identical center in Calcutta was a waste of resources and a duplication of effort, especially since the Serampore mission already had established a missionary center in Calcutta from which Hindu Christians shared the gospel message with other Hindus. Indeed, the situation raised many questions in the minds of people in Serampore and Calcutta. William hoped that people would just ignore it all and not be upset or confused by it. But there were those who could not ignore it, and the strange goings-on among the missionaries became a regular subject of gossip.

Despite the situation among the missionaries, the British rulers of India realized the value of missionary work. Missionaries opened schools, translated documents, and were mostly a peaceful presence wherever they went. Lord Hastings, the new governor-general of India, invited William Carey and Joshua Marshman to dinner to discuss with them sending missionaries to Rajputana. About the same time, Sir David Ochterlony, commercial resident for the newly opened up areas in the foothills of the Himalayas, wrote begging for missionaries to be sent there.

For the first time in all his years in India, William Carey was in the strange position of being in high demand by government officials, even while he was being ignored by the younger missionaries and the missionary society he had helped found back in England. It was a bitter turn of events, and one that upset him more than anything else he'd had to endure in his life. He was especially saddened when he was accused of gathering personal riches. Nothing was further from the truth. Yes, he was paid well for his work as a professor at Fort William College, but all the money he earned was ploughed back into the work of the mission. From the day he left England, William had only ever received six hundred pounds from the missionary society for his personal support. In return, he had given the mission at least forty thousand pounds, which in 1817 was a fortune. William gave more money to the Baptist Missionary Society in India than any other person anywhere in the world. And William had given the mission not only money but also virtually all his time and talent over the past twenty-four years. For some reason, the members of the committee in England had not added up the accounts to see the plain truth for themselves.

Regarding the situation, William wrote to his son Jabez, "Nothing I ever met with in my life—and I have met with many distressing things—ever preyed so much upon my spirit as this difference."

Still, William Carey, Joshua Marshman, and William Ward plodded on in Serampore. Jabez and Mary Carey returned from Amboyna Island, which had been claimed by the Dutch at the end of the Napoleonic War in Europe, and volunteered to go to Rajputana. At the same time, William Ward's son began missionary work on the island of Sumatra in the Dutch East Indies.

William was still worried about Felix, though. Every six months or so he received a letter from his son. As far as he could tell, Felix was still wandering around Assam gathering botany samples and learning new languages.

Finally, in 1818, on a trip east to the Chittagong missionary station, William Ward met up with Felix and persuaded him to return to Serampore. Everyone was delighted to see him when he arrived, and there was plenty of work for him to do. Felix spoke Bengali like a native and was soon put to work supervising the mission's latest project, producing newspapers and magazines. There were three publications. The first was a monthly magazine called *Dig-Darshan,* which meant "the signpost." It was for schoolchildren and was filled with interesting articles about animals, adventurers, explorers, and current events. Many schools in India ordered copies for their students, and soon the mission was printing three thousand copies a month. The second project was the *Samachar Darpan* (news mirror). This was the first newspaper ever to be published in an Asian language, and it too was very popular.

Neither *Dig-Darshan* nor *Samachar Darpan* carried many articles about Christianity. The missionaries in Serampore were concerned about both the educational and the spiritual welfare of the Indian people. Thus, they believed that anything that made people think and understand more about the world around them would also challenge them to look more closely at their own lives, including their religious beliefs.

The third publication was more openly Christian. It was written in English and was called *Friend of India*. Inside the magazine were articles of general interest and a lot of news about what was going on in the country. William Carey used the magazine to remind people about the horrors of the practice of sati and child sacrifice. Although infanticide had been officially outlawed for nearly twenty years, it was still secretly practiced in some places. What bothered William more was that sati was still legal in a country under British rule. William wrote articles telling how brides as young as eleven years of age were being forced onto their husband's funeral pyre. (Girls this young may not have even met their husbands yet. They had been "married" by their parents when they were three or four years old to husbands they would go to live with when they reached childbearing age. Often the husband's family insisted the bride be burned to death so that she would have no claim on her husband's property.)

Felix loved working with William Ward. Together they made a great team. In his spare time, Felix translated *Pilgrim's Progress* and *A History of British India and of England* into Bengali. His father used the books in his classes at Fort William College.

With Felix Carey back at Serampore, William Ward felt free to travel back to England for a break. It was the first time he had returned to England in twenty years. He planned to meet with the missionary society committee while in England and explain the situation in Serampore. He was hopeful that this would help to smooth out some of the difficulties that existed between the missionaries and the missionary society.

While William Ward was away, William Carey and Joshua Marshman set about bringing their next dream to life. Since his early days with Dr. Thomas, William Carey had dreamed of a college similar to Fort William College, but for Indians. There were already two colleges for Indians in Calcutta, one for Hindus and one for Moslems, but William wanted to start a college for Christians to attend. Until this time, a Christian student was not allowed to enroll in either of the other colleges. By now, about six hundred Indians had become Christian converts and had been baptized by William. William was anxious for many of these converts to continue their education, especially learning Sanskrit, so that they could talk intelligently about the gospel message with other educated Indians.

William wanted Serampore College, as he named it, to be a place where Christians from every denomination would feel welcome. This, however, brought him into disagreement again with the missionary society committee back in England. The committee reminded William and Joshua Marshman that it was the *Baptist* Missionary Society and had sent out Baptist missionaries to begin Baptist churches and schools. Back in England, William Ward was able to smooth out the disagreement a little, but the committee could see no value in supporting an interdenominational college.

The Danish people in Serampore understood better than his English "support team" what William Carey was trying to do. The king of Denmark, who carefully followed the work of the Serampore mission, donated five acres of land adjacent to the mission on which to build the college. Soon after, Lord Hastings agreed to be a patron of the college and gave one hundred twenty-five pounds to the building fund. The British government even agreed to pay the cost of hiring a professor of medicine.

William Ward finally arrived back in India with five thousand pounds he had collected from Christians in Great Britain and America. (The Baptist Missionary Society had not approved of his asking Baptists for money for the new college, but many Baptists had given to him privately anyway.)

Despite all his other duties and the responsibilities of starting a new college, William had desired for a long time to do one other thing. He wanted to establish a society to help Indian people better use their farmland to feed more people. He had often spoken to Lady Hastings about this desire, since she shared his love of plants. She encouraged him to do it, and so in 1820, William Carey founded the Agri-Horticultural Society of India. Lady Hastings signed up as the new society's first member. William and Charlotte loved to host the society's meetings in their home. It was exciting for them to meet with other people who loved the flowers and trees of India as much as they did.

At fifty-nine years of age, it may have looked to outsiders that it was time for William Carey to slow down and enjoy old age. But not William. He had struggled against huge obstacles all his life, and the struggle was not yet over.

Chapter 17

# Say Nothing about William Carey

Charlotte Carey had never been strong. Since being seriously burned at age fifteen, she had not been expected to live a long life. Even after she and William had married, most people thought she would live for only a year or two at best. But her love for William had given her new reason to live, and during their years of marriage, she enjoyed reasonably good health.

William loved Charlotte, and the two of them spent as much time together as they could. Like him, she was gifted in languages and read through all his translations, offering helpful suggestions.

By Christmas 1820, however, Charlotte's health was beginning to fail. Each day, William would lovingly carry her out into the garden, where they would sit together for an hour or so talking and praying. On May 30, 1821, Charlotte died. It was the saddest day of William Carey's life. The two of them had been married for thirteen years and three weeks, and William missed Charlotte terribly.

Three more deaths quickly followed Charlotte's. Krishna Pal, the mission's first convert, died of cholera. He had been a strong and energetic evangelist up until the week he died. Next came the death of thirty-seven-year-old Felix Carey as a result of liver problems. Soon afterward, William Ward contracted cholera and died within twenty-four hours. At fifty-four, he was the youngest of the Serampore Triad and the first to die. He had been a faithful and valued member of the team. William mourned the passing of each of them.

In 1823, William married for the third time. His new wife was Grace Hughes, a forty-five-year-old widow. She was kind and generous, and everyone at the Serampore mission was glad when she came to live there.

The two of them had been married only a few months when William injured his thigh in a bad fall while stepping out of his boat. When the governor-general heard of the accident, he immediately sent his private doctor to treat William. The doctor did the best he could according to what was known about medicine in 1823. William's treatment included having one hundred ten bloodsucking leeches placed on his thigh. In spite of the "treatment," William made a slow recovery, and it was six months before he was able to walk again.

Just as when he had injured his foot jumping from the buggy, William had to be carried to and from his lectures at Fort William College.

William's injury was much better by the end of 1823, and William would soon need a good pair of legs to run for his life! The year had been particularly wet, and since almost all of the Bengal region is a huge delta crisscrossed with rivers and swamps, the whole area had begun to flood. The flooded streams and rivers had grown more and more wild until thousands of dead animals and huge trees were tumbling down the Hooghly River in front of the mission. Finally, the river flooded into the mission center and, in the process, washed away William's house. William was home at the time and had to race out of the house to safety to avoid being washed downriver with it. With the house, the garden that had given him and Charlotte so much joy was also washed away.

As the floodwaters receded, the missionaries could see the heavy damage the flood had inflicted on the mission buildings. Just as he had after the print shop fire, William stood in the midst of the ruins and made plans to rebuild. The next day, he sent off a letter to England to order more bulbs and seeds so that he could replant the garden. To provide some extra money for the rebuilding of the mission, he took on the job of translating government documents into Bengali.

Eventually, everything was replaced, and Serampore College was back up and running. Then in 1827, the king of Denmark granted the college the right for all its departments to confer degrees. This was a great honor, as Serampore College was the first college in India to be granted this right. The irony of the situation was not lost on William. He smiled to himself as he recalled how years before he had encouraged dissenter ministers in Kettering to expect great things from God and to achieve great things for God. Now here he was, a man with nothing more than a grade-school education, heading the first college in India granted the right to confer degrees.

The following year, the new governor-general, Lord Bentick, decided to take a serious look at the practice of sati. William had done everything he could to keep the horrible practice in the public eye ever since he had written his report for Lord Wellesley in 1802. Indeed, he had nagged every governor-general since then to make it illegal. Now, finally, it seemed that someone had the courage to do just that.

On Friday, December 4, 1829, Lord Bentick signed an order declaring the practice of sati illegal in all of India. It was two days later, on Sunday morning, that William first read the order. Lord Bentick had sent a copy of it to William and had asked him to translate it into Bengali so that it could be made public. William was so excited he wasted no time. He asked one of the other missionaries to preach the sermon at church that morning, and then he set to work translating the order. He worked as fast as he could. He did not want to waste a single minute, since every minute that passed could mean the death of another widow. He worked all day without even stopping to eat, and by nightfall, the governor-general's messenger was on his way back to Calcutta with the Bengali translation of the order.

Over the next few years, William had more difficulties to face. The banks in India failed, and all the money the mission had was lost. As a result of the financial crisis, Fort William College was forced to close, depriving William of the income that had kept much of the Serampore mission running. Then there was another flood. Once again, William's garden was washed away, and huge mahogany trees, swept along by the river, crashed through his greenhouses, shattering them into a thousand pieces. As soon as the floodwaters receded, William began planting a new garden yet again.

William also plodded on through another revision of the Bengali New Testament and lectured in religion and science at Serampore College. Even though he was now an old man, he remained faithful to the call of being a missionary. He would never give up that call or retire from it.

In July 1833, William suffered a stroke. Although he did recover a little, it was soon followed by another stroke and then another. Each stroke left him weaker than the one before. Despite the effects of the strokes, William loved to be in his garden and so was carried out there every day. In the end, however, being carried outside became too stressful for him. The gardener would bring flowers and leaves into William's room and talk to William about how each plant was doing.

William's three surviving sons also came to be with him. Jabez came from Rajputana, where he was still running a mission station; William Jr. came from Cutwa, where he was doing the same. Jonathan, now thirty-seven years old, came up from Calcutta, where he was a well-known attorney. Many other people came to visit him as well, including the governor-general and his wife; Dr. Wilson, the bishop of Calcutta; and other newly arrived missionaries.

One of the last people to visit William was Alexander Duff. He had come to discuss his own plans to establish a Christian college in India, and William encouraged him. Alexander Duff was deeply impressed with William's years of missionary service in India and talked to him about them also. But since William tired easily, he did not want to stay too long. As he started to walk toward the door, though, William sat up in bed and called him back. "Mr. Duff," he said in a feeble voice, "you have been speaking about William Carey. When I am gone, say nothing about William Carey—speak only about William Carey's Savior."

In the early hours of June 9, 1834, William Carey died quietly in his bed. He was seventy-two years old. In his will, he asked to be buried next to his second wife, Charlotte. He directed that a simple headstone was to be placed on his grave. The headstone was to give his name and age, under which was to be inscribed, "A wretched, poor, and helpless worm. On Thy kind arms I fall."

William Carey may have seen himself as poor and wretched, but people saw him as something quite different. As his body was carried through the streets of Serampore, the flags at the Danish Government House were lowered to half staff. And the streets were lined with silent crowds of Hindus, Moslems, and Christians, all wanting one last look at the man who had become a well-loved legend in the Bengal region.

William Carey, the man who began life as the son of a poor weaver, had taught himself Latin, Hebrew, and Greek as he worked as a cordwainer. When he became convinced that England should be sending out missionaries to newly opened up countries, he helped found the first English missionary society. He then felt obliged to go to India as its first missionary. When difficult circumstances surrounded him—he watched his children die and wife go insane—he never lost faith. He always endured, always pressed ahead. In the process, he founded the most prestigious college of its time in India. He translated the Bible into many Indian and Asian languages. He helped start numerous churches and schools around India. He spoke out against inhuman practices, and he never once wavered in his calling to share the gospel message with Indian people wherever he found them.

In the course of his life, William Carey set a pattern and a standard for missionary work that in the years since his death, many have copied, but few have matched.

## *Bibliography*

Drewery, Mary. *William Carey*. Zondervan, 1978.

Finnie, Kellsye M. *William Carey*. Christian Literature Crusade, 1986.

Miller, Basil. *William Carey: The Father of Modern Missions*. Bethany House Publishers, 1980.

Smith, George. *The Life of William Carey: Shoemaker and Missionary*. E. P. Dutton

Walker, F. Deaville. *William Carey: Missionary Pioneer and Statesman*. Moody Press, 1925.

## *About the Authors*

Janet and Geoff Benge are a husband and wife writing team with more than thirty years of writing experience. Janet is a former elementary school teacher. Geoff holds a degree in history. Originally from New Zealand, the Benges spent ten years serving with Youth With A Mission. They have two daughters, Laura and Shannon, and an adopted son, Lito. They make their home in the Orlando, Florida, area.

CHRISTIAN HEROES: THEN & NOW are available in paperback, e-book, and audiobook formats, with more coming soon!

**www.HeroesThenAndNow.com**

# *Also from Janet and Geoff Benge...*

More adventure-filled biographies for ages 10 to 100!

## Christian Heroes: Then and Now

*Gladys Aylward: The Adventure of a Lifetime • 978-1-57658-019-6*
*Nate Saint: On a Wing and a Prayer • 978-1-57658-017-2*
*Hudson Taylor: Deep in the Heart of China • 978-1-57658-016-5*
*Amy Carmichael: Rescuer of Precious Gems • 978-1-57658-018-9*
*Eric Liddell: Something Greater Than Gold • 978-1-57658-137-7*
*Corrie ten Boom: Keeper of the Angels' Den • 978-1-57658-136-0*
*William Carey: Obliged to Go • 978-1-57658-147-6*
*George Müller: Guardian of Bristol's Orphans • 978-1-57658-145-2*
*Jim Elliot: One Great Purpose • 978-1-57658-146-9*
*Mary Slessor: Forward into Calabar • 978-1-57658-148-3*
*David Livingstone: Africa's Trailblazer • 978-1-57658-153-7*
*Betty Greene: Wings to Serve • 978-1-57658-152-0*
*Adoniram Judson: Bound for Burma • 978-1-57658-161-2*
*Cameron Townsend: Good News in Every Language • 978-1-57658-164-3*
*Jonathan Goforth: An Open Door in China • 978-1-57658-174-2*
*Lottie Moon: Giving Her All for China • 978-1-57658-188-9*
*John Williams: Messenger of Peace • 978-1-57658-256-5*
*William Booth: Soup, Soap, and Salvation • 978-1-57658-258-9*
*Rowland Bingham: Into Africa's Interior • 978-1-57658-282-4*
*Ida Scudder: Healing Bodies, Touching Hearts • 978-1-57658-285-5*
*Wilfred Grenfell: Fisher of Men • 978-1-57658-292-3*
*Lillian Trasher: The Greatest Wonder in Egypt • 978-1-57658-305-0*
*Loren Cunningham: Into All the World • 978-1-57658-199-5*
*Florence Young: Mission Accomplished • 978-1-57658-313-5*
*Sundar Singh: Footprints Over the Mountains • 978-1-57658-318-0*
*C.T. Studd: No Retreat • 978-1-57658-288-6*
*Rachel Saint: A Star in the Jungle • 978-1-57658-337-1*
*Brother Andrew: God's Secret Agent • 978-1-57658-355-5*
*Clarence Jones: Mr. Radio • 978-1-57658-343-2*
*Count Zinzendorf: Firstfruit • 978-1-57658-262-6*
*John Wesley: The World His Parish • 978-1-57658-382-1*
*C. S. Lewis: Master Storyteller • 978-1-57658-385-2*
*David Bussau: Facing the World Head-on • 978-1-57658-415-6*
*Jacob DeShazer: Forgive Your Enemies • 978-1-57658-475-0*
*Isobel Kuhn: On the Roof of the World • 978-1-57658-497-2*
*Elisabeth Elliot: Joyful Surrender • 978-1-57658-513-9*
*D. L. Moody: Bringing Souls to Christ • 978-1-57658-552-8*
*Paul Brand: Helping Hands • 978-1-57658-536-8*
*Dietrich Bonhoeffer: In the Midst of Wickedness • 978-1-57658-713-3*
*Francis Asbury: Circuit Rider • 978-1-57658-737-9*
*Samuel Zwemer: The Burden of Arabia • 978-1-57658-738-6*

*Klaus-Dieter John: Hope in the Land of the Incas* • 978-1-57658-826-2
*Mildred Cable: Through the Jade Gate* • 978-1-57658-886-4
*John Flynn: Into the Never Never* • 978-1-57658-898-7
*Richard Wurmbrand: Love Your Enemies* • 978-1-57658-987-8
*Charles Mulli: We Are Family* • 978-1-57658-894-9
*John Newton: Change of Heart* • 978-1-57658-909-0
*Helen Roseveare: Mama Luka* • 978-1-57658-910-6
*Norman Grubb: Mission Builder* • 978-1-57658-915-1
*Albert Schweitzer* • 978-1-57658-961-8

## Heroes of History

*George Washington Carver: From Slave to Scientist* • 978-1-883002-78-7
*Abraham Lincoln: A New Birth of Freedom* • 978-1-883002-79-4
*Meriwether Lewis: Off the Edge of the Map* • 978-1-883002-80-0
*George Washington: True Patriot* • 978-1-883002-81-7
*William Penn: Liberty and Justice for All* • 978-1-883002-82-4
*Harriet Tubman: Freedombound* • 978-1-883002-90-9
*John Adams: Independence Forever* • 978-1-883002-50-3
*Clara Barton: Courage under Fire* • 978-1-883002-51-0
*Daniel Boone: Frontiersman* • 978-1-932096-09-5
*Theodore Roosevelt: An American Original* • 978-1-932096-10-1
*Douglas MacArthur: What Greater Honor* • 978-1-932096-15-6
*Benjamin Franklin: Live Wire* • 978-1-932096-14-9
*Christopher Columbus: Across the Ocean Sea* • 978-1-932096-23-1
*Laura Ingalls Wilder: A Storybook Life* • 978-1-932096-32-3
*Orville Wright: The Flyer* • 978-1-932096-34-7
*Captain John Smith: A Foothold in the New World* • 978-1-932096-36-1
*Thomas Edison: Inspiration and Hard Work* • 978-1-932096-37-8
*Alan Shepard: Higher and Faster* • 978-1-932096-41-5
*Ronald Reagan: Destiny at His Side* • 978-1-932096-65-1
*Davy Crockett: Ever Westward* • 978-1-932096-67-5
*Milton Hershey: More Than Chocolate* • 978-1-932096-82-8
*Billy Graham: America's Pastor* • 978-1-62486-024-9
*Ben Carson: A Chance at Life* • 978-1-62486-034-8
*Louis Zamperini: Redemption* • 978-1-62486-049-2
*Elizabeth Fry: Angel of Newgate* • 978-1-62486-064-5
*William Wilberforce: Take Up the Fight* • 978-1-62486-057-7
*William Bradford: Plymouth's Rock* • 978-1-62486-092-8
*Ernest Shackleton: Going South* • 978-1-62486-093-5
*Benjamin Rush: The Common Good* • 978-1-62486-123-9
*Dwight Eisenhower: Supreme Commander* • 978-1-62486-142-0
*Frederick Douglass: The Right to Dignity* • 978-1-62486-151-2
*Winston Chruchill: Resolute* • 978-1-62486-153-6